Relationship Recovery

The Couple Therapist

Relationship Recovery Workbook

Powerful, Fast and Effective Strategies for your Relationship

Contact:

www.bayviewpractice.co.uk

FIRST EDITION

This book is dedicated to my family who have

given me so much love and support in life

and in loving memory of my father.

A man whose courage and determination

impacted many lives including mine

in a positive and inspiring way.

Contents

Acknowledgements

First and foremost, I would like to thank and acknowledge the clients I have worked with throughout the years. Your courage, persistence and willingness to look at yourselves as well as your relationship, never cease to amaze and inspire me. Without you, this book could not have been written.

It is a huge privilege to have been part of your process.

My grateful thanks also go to Carol for all your hard work in proofing and editing this book. Your meticulous eye for detail and experience lies behind this final manuscript. Thank you for your advice and constant support throughout. They have been invaluable.

To Caroline @caroillustrate. Thank you for ensuring that my vision was realised. Always being reliable and professional throughout. Your work was delivered on time and you came up with some great ideas when I was unsure of which direction to go in.

To Chris, for always being so accommodating, professional and efficient. Thank you for putting everything together and enabling this book to be published in a polished and professional way.

To Andy, for your informed advice and for taking the time to answer all my questions so thoroughly.

To everyone who very kindly took the time to read this book and give your constructive feedback. It is much appreciated.

Lastly but by no means least, I would also like to thank my family, friends and colleagues for their encouragement and support in writing this book. Reading through my drafts, giving me supportive words as well as your honest feedback. Keeping me fed and watered whilst working as a full-time therapist, has made this book possible.

Introduction

'You will never know unless you try...'

Are you unhappy or lonely in your relationship?

It does not have to be that way.

You can have a happy and fulfilling relationship.

This book will help reveal what ingredients are needed to create a relationship that fulfils both of your needs. It will give you a better understanding of yourself and your partner. In the following pages, I will teach you various tools so that you can identify and work on the issues that trouble and strain your relationship. Whether you are recovering from an affair, have problems communicating with each other or lack intimacy in your relationship, 'The Relationship Recovery Workbook' has proven, powerful strategies and tools to help you get the best out of your partnership.

Counselling is highly effective in helping couples to resolve issues within their relationship, but it is not always available or accessible to all. If therapy is not an option for you due to finances, location or personal choice but you would like to have the additional professional support, this book will be the closest thing to being in a session and working with me. In the following chapters, we will be working together through the various issues you have in your relationship. With proven and effective exercises along the way, you will be able to understand and see how to change the communication and dynamics resulting in a powerful and positive shift within your relationship.

'The Relationship Recovery Workbook' was written with a view to be accessible to everyone and to reflect the way I work in my practice. An easy to read, straightforward, no-nonsense approach that takes into consideration that most of us live busy and demanding lives.

Throughout this book, I will use examples of clients I have worked with and will give you practical and insightful ways of looking at and dealing with your own problems and situations. I will also challenge the behaviours and thoughts that are present in your relationship.

During the clients' first session, I highlight that the work in the therapy room is only part of the process, the other key part is applying the knowledge to the relationship as soon as they walk out of the practice room. The same applies to reading this book. Reading this book is not enough, if only life were that simple! You have to be willing to do the exercises, reflect and take action where needed. Most of us lead very busy lives but if you were to take note of the number of hours spent arguing, being unhappy, sad or lonely, then the time spent on these exercises is time well spent and the results can have an immediate positive impact on your relationship.

This is an interactive book. The more you put in, the more you will get out of it. It is helpful to do the exercises by writing them down. This is quite different to answering them in your head as writing them down cements thoughts enabling you to retain them better and be able to reflect on your words, thoughts and feelings. It will also act as a reference guide as you progress, so you will both be able to see just how far your relationship, thoughts and behaviours have changed through this process.

If you are able to do the exercises together, great. But this book can also help you should your partner not be ready or willing to join you at this stage. Use your newfound awareness and apply it to your relationship. Any changes that you make can also impact the relationship in a positive way. These are simple but effective tools. I have my clients' positive feedback as proof that this works. Doing the exercises will increase your awareness of the part that you play as well as look at your relationship as a whole.

We all live our lives through our own set of 'lenses'. Some may look at life through a positive lens and look for the positive things in life. Others may look at life through a very cautious and protective lens, having been hurt in the past. The way you look at life or through your own personal lens is determined by your life script. In other words, the way you were brought up.

Our experiences in life and our genes all influence how we see and react to situations, events and people on a daily basis. An example of this is when two people experience the same thing but have a very different take on the same situation. Take finances for example. One partner may have been brought up with very little money and associate a lack of money with unhappiness, feelings of shame or going hungry and so be very cautious and want to save money in adult life. Their partner may have also been brought up in an environment where money was scarce but for them, they see money as there to be spent, living in the moment, freedom and happiness. These are very different ways of approaching money and can cause a lot of resentment, arguments and heartache between a couple if not understood and looked at.

Viewing life in a certain way does not necessarily make it 'right or wrong', the key here is to develop a better understanding and awareness (my favourite word!) to enable you to look at the issues with clarity in order to make the changes needed within your relationship.

There also needs to be a willingness to see ourselves as we really are and what part we play in the relationship. This can be an uncomfortable but necessary process and where courage comes in. It is much easier to focus on what your partner is doing wrong than to look at what we could do to change the dynamics within the relationship.

This book is for everyone of all genders and cultural backgrounds. With different ways of being with regards to relationships. Whether you have a monogamous relationship, same sex marriage or an open marriage and you want your relationship to be the best it can be, this book is for you.

Important note about abuse:

Physical and mental abuse has no place in relationships. This book is not here to help you to deal with or accept abuse. If you are unsure whether you are in an abusive relationship or how to cope in this situation, please seek help from appropriate agencies or professionals today.

Please note that all client's names and identifying features have been changed in all the examples and case studies.

I look forward to working with you and will help and support you throughout this book so that you can have a better understanding of yourself as well as your partnership.

Chapter 1

The Assessment

'Where your relationship has arrived is a result of the journey it took to get there'

Why work at your relationship?

Many people come to counselling or reach out for help when their relationship is at breaking point. At this stage, both parties are usually exhausted, emotionally and physically, making the reparatory work more difficult. Some couples may want to throw in the towel as it feels like 'too much work, too tiring, too late', only subsequently to then look back and wish they had tried harder and given their relationship the attention it needed.

Are you ready to commit to your relationship? Is your partner?

I am referring to you taking the time out to read this book. Even ten minutes a day will make a big difference.

You need to take the time to ponder, reflect and take action where needed. We live in a quick fix society and we want quick fixes, don't we? But a relationship takes time to take shape and grow. This applies to healing or repairing it too. You will be able to see some changes straight away and others may need practice and consistency in order for you to feel confident and trust in the changes being made.

You need to set aside time for your relationship. Excuses will not change it. If you have time to brush your teeth or shower – you have time to work on your relationship!

You only have one life. Why settle for less than you both deserve? Unless you decide today that you want, need and deserve a better relationship, you will remain in the same relationship with the same issues. If it were good enough for you, I doubt you would be reading this book.

How powerful is it to know that you are both able to make the changes necessary to be in a happy and healthy relationship?

I have seen my clients' relationships change drastically with a few small, consistent but crucial changes. So, if you would like to understand how you arrived at where you are in your relationship and where to go from here, please read the book in its entirety. Then, make the changes necessary so that you are able to live the life you both deserve.

You may wish to read through the book first and then go back and work through each chapter, doing the exercises at your own pace. You can, of course, jump chapters to the ones you feel are relevant to you or as a couple, but you may then be missing out on crucial work needed to build the foundations of your relationship. How many times have I heard a couple say 'Oh, we are fine with communication, finances are the issue'. Only to discover during the sessions that communication, or lack of, was the problem behind the tensions relating to finances.

Both parties are not always able or willing to partake in talking or making the changes needed. It is important not to underestimate the changes that can occur when only one person is looking at their behaviours and actions within the relationship. The changes one person makes in a relationship can really impact how their partner behaves towards them, how they respond and their general way of being within the relationship. One positive change, whether as an individual or as a couple, can have a real 'domino' effect and other positive changes can then ensue.

In my first session with a couple, I do an assessment of the relationship. Assessments are basically a set of questions to evaluate and gather information about your relationship in order to be able to identify the initial problems and to look at the best interventions needed at this stage. It offers an overview of the couple's life, outside influences and anything else that can impact the individual and the couple.

Now, let's have a look at your relationship.

Exercise

The following exercise will start to give you an overall outline of your relationship. Remember to write your answers down as this will help the overall process:

* How did you meet?
* What attracted you to one another when you first met?
* What kept you together after that first initial meeting/attraction?
* How long have you been together?

* What difficulties and challenges have you had to face in your relationship? (For example: financial difficulties, loss of a loved one, an affair, health issues).
* When did you start noticing issues in your relationship?
* What were the telling signs that all was not well in the relationship?
* What is your communication like? (Both practical as in 'we need more milk' and emotional 'I feel sad when you say...')
* What is your affection, intimacy, sex life like?
* What is your support system like? (Family, friends, therapist)

If you have carried on reading and skipped this exercise, I would urge you to find a quiet moment and go back to answer the questions as they are the foundation for the following chapters. We will be looking at some of the above topics in more depth later in the book.

The exercise above is invaluable in getting a better understanding of your couple history and the journey you both took leading you to where you are today. Even if you think, 'Well that's easy, I know where we are today. My partner had an affair, that says it all'. It is important for you both to understand root causes, beliefs, and ways of being. In this example, to either work on your relationship and ensure this never happens again or make the informed decision to part ways.

Once you have done the exercise, read it back to yourself. If you can, read it in a factual rather than emotional way. What you are doing, is informing yourself about your relationship. It is important that, at this stage, emotions do not take over. If there is a lot of anger or resentment, you may focus on one issue that causes you distress and miss the point of the exercise, which is to really look at the answers and your relationship as a whole.

Well done on completing the first exercise. You are already closer to having a happier and more fulfilling relationship in your life.

It takes courage to make the decision to look at your relationship and reach out for support. You want to find a way forward. To be able to go forward you need to know what you are moving forward from. The quick and easy answer may be 'because they did this or said that...' But life is not that one-dimensional. In my experience, it is never 'just' this or that. I have yet to meet a couple where both parties had nothing to be aware of, look at, challenge or change about themselves. We all have things we can work on and challenge about ourselves as individuals and as a couple.

You may feel that you are a very attentive, caring and selfless partner and therefore do not need to look at your part in the relationship. If you are attentive, caring and selfless in your relationship, would it be helpful to look at boundaries for example. Do you feel appreciated? Do you feel taken for granted? Do you live your life through your partner? These are all things that would need to be looked at to ensure that the behaviours in the relationship are healthy and fair for both parties. Whether that means creating better boundaries for yourself as an individual or challenging some of your behaviours within the relationship.

Try to be as honest as you can without 'editing' yourself and write down the following answers. (By editing, I am referring to feeling that, at times, we should not say certain things or think in a certain way. Just write what you really feel inside)

Exercise

Do this exercise as individuals first and set your answers aside. Look back at the answers together once you have completed the chapter on Communication.

* What do you currently like about your partner?
* What do you currently dislike about your partner?
* What do you feel are the issues in your relationship?
* Do you feel these are entirely your partner's fault?
* If not, what part do you feel you play?
* What behaviours of your partner contribute to these issues?
* What beliefs of your partner contribute to these issues?
* Was it a slow erosion or a single event that affected your relationship?

What you are starting to do, is to create a relationship map.

Some of these questions may be uncomfortable to answer. Some may be easy and some more difficult, but it is by asking yourself these questions that you will be able to open up your way of thinking regarding your relationship. When we are unhappy in our situation, we tend to focus and at times, even obsess over the problem. In the same way that blinkers obscure a horse's vision for example, this can 'blinker' our thoughts, our awareness, our understanding and, therefore, the solutions too as we only focus on the problem.

Exercise

How do you show your partner that you love them?

* With **words** (I love you, you are amazing…)
* With **actions** (making sure you cook a favourite meal of theirs, looking after the children so they can take a break)
* With **affection** and being tactile (being physically demonstrative with kisses, hugs, intimacy)

How does your partner show their love for you?

* With **words** (I love you, you are amazing…)
* With **actions** (making sure they cook a favourite meal of yours, looking after the children so you can take a break)
* With **affection** and being tactile (being physically demonstrative with kisses, hugs, intimacy)

In the sessions, some couples struggle to answer this question. If you feel that the answer is 'nothing', then write down ways in which they used to show it in the past. If you feel it is a mixture of all of them, is there one that dominates and stands out?

Now, having done the exercise, take a moment to look at how you show your partner that you love them and how they show you that they love you.

Is it the same or different? How we show our love to one another is usually how we like to receive it. So, what happens if you are both different? What if your partner is doing their utmost to do as much as they can so that you feel loved? They cook a special meal, pick up the shopping and put up the shelf in the bathroom you have been talking about. But what if your need is for affection? Despite all their efforts, you may still not feel loved.

Part of the issue is that you and your partner may not notice how you show each other love. If you show your love through affection, chances are that you will want or even need affection back to feel loved.

So, what is the solution? The first step is recognising that even though it may not be how **you** show and would like to be shown love, it is about appreciating and recognising your **partner's** way of showing you love.

* Taking the bins out when it is your turn = I love you
* Giving you a hug when you are feeling down = I love you
* Running a bath for when you get home = I love you
* 'Thank you for everything you do' = I love you
* Taking you out for a meal = I love you

The second step is for your partner to recognise how **you** like to be shown love and gift it to you. Giving you a hug or saying loving things may not be how they naturally show you their love, but it is important that they consider your needs and wants and vice versa. Some clients fear that it may be forced and unnatural, but I have found that couples tend to feel very positively about their relationship when putting the above into practice. They start appreciating each other more and the positive response they get when they gift a hug, a cup of tea or an 'I love you' has a knock-on effect. They then want and choose to gift and appreciate each other more and the couple is closer as a result.

Notice my use of the word 'gift' because that is what it is, 'a gift' for your partner.

It goes without saying that you need to be authentic in your actions and words. You are not merely 'ticking a box', you are showing each other that you are considering each other's needs and that you love each other.

Patting your partner on the back as you would a pet whilst counting the seconds is not going to feel like receiving a gift, it will feel more like a chore for both partners. So, choose a gift that is genuine for you too.

Exercise

Once you have discovered how you show love, see if you can notice what your partner is and has been doing to show you love. Now that you both know each other's needs, what could you 'gift' one another?

Important note: If you do not feel that your relationship is ready for this exercise, please continue to work through this book and come back to it when you are both in a better place.

For most of us, life is lived in a busy, stressful, and fast-paced world. Most couples say that they struggle to find ten minutes of peace in a day, let alone have time for fun. And yet when I ask how much fun they had when they were dating, we are looking at a whole other story! 'Fun was more of a priority back then' I hear them say…**They** were more of a priority back then.

It always surprises couples of young families when I highlight the importance of putting themselves first before their children. Now, let me make it clear that I am not referring to the child's welfare, essential care and needs. These need to take priority. No, I am talking about couples who, when dating, would ensure that the relationship's needs were catered for and were a priority and now, the couple is not a priority at all. They would happily spend all weekend picking up and dropping off their children to and from clubs or playdates but not ensure that they include some time as a couple too.

For a lot of couples, priorities change drastically as time goes by. Whether you have a young family, a demanding job or an all-consuming pastime, your relationship may have slipped down the order of importance. Sadly, for some, it can come after shopping, housework or DIY and be at the bottom of their priorities as opposed to at the top.

'This therapist does not live in the real world, it's totally unrealistic. I don't have five minutes to myself, let alone time for us as a couple' and yet…. when I challenge my clients and ask them whether they would find time for a regular medical appointment for themselves or a child… they all, without exception, say they would 100% be there. So, we went from impossible to definite in one change of perspective!

Another argument I am given is that it is not morally right to put children after the couple's needs. My question is this then:

'If the couple are arguing or are living in a toxic environment, does this not impact the couple and the children in a negative way?'

For the sake of the couple and the children, it is vital to look at your relationship, whether you decide you would like to work at it or part ways.

Chapter 2

The roles that we play

'One of the most difficult and courageous things to do in a relationship, is to look at the part we play in it'

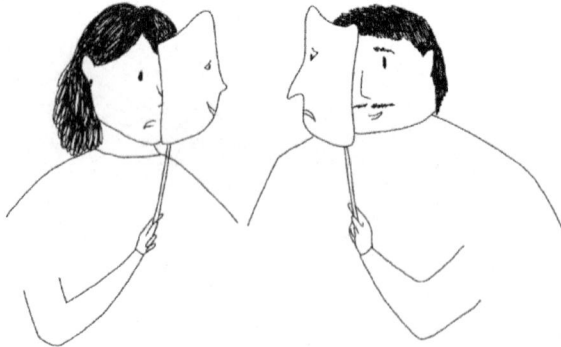

What roles do you play in your relationship?

In this chapter, we are going to look at the roles you play in your relationship. What you say and how you say it, your behaviours within the relationship and how this impacts you as a couple.

Now that you have your relationship template from having done the exercises in the first chapter, you can start looking at the roles both of you play and your contribution to the relationship.

One of the hardest things to do is to have a look at the part we play in our relationship. It is so much easier and more comfortable to highlight the other person's flaws and wrongdoings than to look at how our actions and ways of being have impacted our partner. Some things may seem obvious, but some may need more self-reflection, with, at times, a dose of humility as it is not always easy to look at ourselves objectively.

Again, the following exercises are applicable to both partners but if your partner is not yet ready to join you at this stage, it can still be beneficial to your relationship for you to do the exercises on your own.

This exercise will help you to reflect on your relationship and your part in it. Exercise A and B need to be completed by both partners where possible or by yourself if applicable:

Exercise A

* If you met your partner today, would you choose to date them? Please give reasons for your answer
* In what ways do you bring happiness to the relationship?
* Do you respect your partner? If yes, in what ways do you show it?
* Do you disrespect your partner? If yes, in what ways do you do this?

* Do you feel your issues are mainly due to outside factors? (For example: work, family, finances)
  If yes, what are the factors and how do they impact the relationship?
* Would being alone with your partner be bliss?
* Are you happy with the intimacy and sex in your relationship?
  If not, what would you like to be different?
* Do you connect and talk to your partner easily?
* What do you talk to your partner about in the main? (Work, children, finances, house issues, fun things...?)
* Do you feel you understand your partner?
  Give some examples of this.
* Do you plan the future together?
  If so, are these plans compatible?
* Do you listen to and support your partner's hopes and dreams?
  If so, in what way do you support them?
* Do you love your partner?
  How do you know this?

Exercise B

The following exercise looks at the role your partner plays in your relationship from your perspective:

* Do you feel that if your partner met you today, they would choose to date you?
  Please give reasons for your answer.
* In what ways does your partner make you happy?
* Do you feel your partner respects you?
  If yes, how do you feel they show this?
* Do you feel your partner disrespects you?
  If yes, please give examples.
* Do you feel your partner is affected by outside factors such as work, family, stress?

If yes, what are the factors and how does this impact your relationship?

* Do you feel your partner is happy with the intimacy and sex in your relationship?

* Do you feel that your partner is able to talk to you easily?

* What does your partner mainly talk to you about (Work, children, finances, house issues or fun things?)

* Do you feel your partner understands you?
  Give examples based on your answer.

* Does your partner listen to and support your hopes and dreams?
  If so, in what ways do they support you?

* Do you feel loved by your partner?
  If so, how do they show you that they love you?

Now that you have a clearer idea of the roles that you play in the relationship, it is best to put the answers to exercises A and B aside until you have completed the book. We will be looking at the issues raised above, such as respect, further on in the book. It is helpful to revisit this exercise at the end of the book when you have acquired the tools needed to deal with any issues or problems that have been highlighted in your answers. Done in this way, it will also highlight the progress made and the changes that have taken place in your relationship.

The aim of these questions is for you to gain more awareness and clarity on your roles in the relationship as well as where your relationship is at this moment in time. When we explore these questions in a session, it can leave clients feeling that their relationship is worse than they realised, but this is a normal reaction. We sometimes put plasters over issues and problems, and it is only when we take the plaster off, face the wound and clean it, that the healing can really take place. The wound being the issue or problem you are facing in your relationship at that time.

Let us use the following example to highlight this.

Say you have had a fight with your partner just before leaving for work. You may decide to suppress your anger (by suppressing the anger, you are putting 'a plaster on the wound' or the issue, but not dealing with it) until you return from work. By the time you return home from work, you may have had an opportunity to process what happened. You may then be able to talk about it together calmly (by talking about the issue, you have 'taken the plaster off the wound'). A resolution or compromise may be found ('You are now cleaning the wound' or sorting the issue out). If you do not feel you can talk about it then the issue stays unprocessed and unresolved (plaster stays over an infected wound). Suppressed emotions as per the example above, are best dealt with when the individual is ready to do so in order to avoid them lingering and being left unprocessed. These suppressed emotions will remain buried only to resurface in arguments at a later date and build up resentment in the process.

Emotions can be challenging to feel and deal with, which is why a lot of clients have got into the habit of not dealing with them, in the hope that they will disappear and fade away by themselves. So, these emotions just sit there and fester waiting for an opportunity such as an (often unrelated) argument to release some of those suppressed emotions. So, you fly off the handle over the toothpaste top being left off when in fact your resentment was really to do with your partner flirting with a colleague at a work's party.

Suppressed emotions are also worth looking at from an individual's health point of view. Suppressed and unprocessed emotions have a strong link to depression and anxiety as your internal being is not free. You carry these unwelcome and uncomfortable feelings everywhere you go.

An additional factor for most of us is the fast-paced life we lead. We 'don't have time to heal, to talk to one another, to process…' Ironically, a lot more time is spent on being mentally exhausted, angry or anxious when you don't process your emotions. Giving your relationship the space to talk and deal with how you are feeling frees you both to focus on having a happy, fun and loving relationship.

You may, however, have repressed emotions. This is different to suppressing them. Repressed emotions are emotions that you unconsciously avoid and therefore they do not usually get dealt with and processed unless you become aware of them. An example of a repressed emotion is a person who was constantly criticised in childhood. As an adult, that person may be particularly sensitive to any form of criticism (real or perceived). The most common emotions that get repressed are frustration, fear, disappointment, sadness, and anger.

Repressed emotions can also be the cause of feeling anxious, stressed or depressed. If this resonates with you in any way, use that newfound awareness when reading this book. As you practise the exercises in the book, ask yourself the question:

'When I have a strong reaction or emotion to an argument or something that is said or highlighted, could it be because of repressed emotions?'

If you have suffered a toxic or abusive childhood, experienced a trauma or an impacting event in your life, you may wish to seek professional help. This book will help your relationship but if you find that your past creates a mental or physical barrier to your happiness, you deserve to get the help you need to free yourself of the pain and lead a happier life as an individual as well as in your relationship.

Understanding each other and what impacts us as individuals is key to a healthy and happy relationship.

When misunderstandings and arguments are frequent in a relationship, one of the exercises that I do with couples early on in therapy to help them understand each other better is the 'empathy exercise'.

Empathy is different to sympathy. It is putting yourself in someone else's shoes. In this case, your partner's shoes, and looking at life through their eyes.

I start by asking each person to describe what they think it is like to be their partner. For ease of understanding, I will use the couple Chris and Sam in this example.

Usually, the person starting the exercise (in this example, Chris) will begin by describing what they think it must be like to be the other partner (Sam).

Very often, the following happens:

* Chris will describe how they feel Sam might be feeling

* Chris will continue but then start talking about themselves instead. Saying how life is unfair for them, how hurt they are. So instead of Chris describing what it is like to be Sam, Chris will then change it to Chris talking about Chris.

I have found that this is one of the hardest exercises for clients to do. To focus on the other person without bringing their own hurts and injustices into it.

When this happens, I stop the exercise and, in this example, would ask Chris to repeat the process. This time, encouraging Chris to look at life through Sam's eyes. Having done this, it is then Sam's turn to do the same exercise, looking at life solely through Chris' eyes.

I then ask each of them if they feel their partner had given a good description of how they were feeling. Did they want to add or change anything that was said? Did they have a genuine understanding what their partner was feeling and going through.

Exercise

Do the exercise above but write it down as opposed to saying it to each other. You will not have me in the room as a mediator to stop the exercise if one of you is not doing the exercise correctly but by writing it down, you will be able to have time to review what you have written and ask yourself – is this partly about me or solely about my partner?

Once you have written it down, take it in turns to do the following:

* Partner **A** – Read what you have written out loud to partner **B**
* Then ask partner **B** if there is anything they would like to add or change
* Partner **B** responds to partner **A**
* Partner **B**, were there any surprises in what partner **A** said about you?
  If yes, in what way?

* Partner **B** – Read what you have written out loud partner **A**
* Then ask partner **A** if there is anything they would like to add or change
* Partner **A** responds to partner **B**
* Partner A, were there any surprises in what partner B said about you?
  If yes, in what way?

If you feel that your relationship is prone to arguments at this time, you may need to approach this with a definite set of boundaries such as keeping to the topic and exercise at hand. Agree to not interrupt each other and to really listen to what your partner says without voicing a judgement on how they feel.

This exercise starts the basis of understanding each other better and empathising with what it feels like to be your partner at this point in time. It is not an excuse to voice your complaints, anger or grievances to your partner as this would not be helpful for you or your relationship.

If you feel your partner has either missed the point or does not understand how it feels to be you at the moment, write down how you feel. Again, we are looking at how you feel. So, for example, saying that you are hurting, not sleeping, feel as though you are grieving and have increased anxiety, is letting your partner understand what it is like to be you at the moment. Saying that you are hurting because they are (name calling) and it's all their fault and what are they going to do about it is not the point of this exercise.

The roles we play in a relationship are largely borne out of our 'life scripts'. In other words, what we have experienced in life thus far and the way we see life. The way we react and respond to words, people and events is due, in part, to our upbringing, influences and experiences growing up. Other things also influence who we are. Our genetic make-up and our current lifestyle, for example.

Below are some examples of how certain events or experiences in our life can impact the relationships we have today:

29

Broken trust: Have you experienced being cheated on in a past relationship? Or being constantly lied to? This may make it difficult to trust anyone. This can result in having one foot in the relationship and one foot out of it. It is difficult to feel totally committed and trust our significant other when we have experienced such hurt. Emotional defence barriers may be created and there may even be mistrust towards a kind act for example, thinking that there is an ulterior motive behind it. Trust can take a while to be rebuilt and so can bringing down the emotional defence barriers that we use to 'protect' us from being hurt. Trouble is, all too often, these very same barriers protect us from love as well as hurt.

Abandonment: Fear of abandonment can have a significant effect on a person's relationship. Abandonment can create a fear of not being important enough or meaning enough to our partners. This in turn may mean that the person with abandonment issues may become a people pleaser to ensure being liked and, therefore, feel that they are less likely to be rejected. One of the issues with this, is that the individual spends so much time moulding themselves to please others, including their partner, that they lose sight of who they really are and what **their** own likes and dislikes are. They may also feel that they need to 'control' their partner so that they can avoid being left by them. Or have a need for frequent reassurance through words, affection or actions.

It can also mean that people with abandonment issues can be attracted to people who are unable to commit.

Criticism: Setting a higher bar for yourself and others. Feeling a constant pressure to be the best and not make mistakes. This, in turn, can put a lot of pressure on the relationship itself. The pressure to be the best can leave a partner feeling left behind. Or the expectations of your significant other can be unrealistic and unforgiving. There can be a real fear of failure too. As an individual and as a couple, of not feeling good enough. Approval from others is often sought. Status and wealth may be seen as a means to achieve this approval.

Receiving criticism within the relationship may be difficult for the individual to take but they may be quick to criticise their partner. This can lead to resentment, misunderstandings, arguments and ultimately, both parties not feeling good enough.

Trauma: Trauma can leave an imprint on an individual's life and can, therefore, affect relationships too. On the surface, a person can continue to lead a functional life, but trauma can affect how we view certain things. It can create triggers for us or affect our mood. You may have experienced a single trauma or a complex trauma (where the trauma has been repeated, such as childhood bullying for example). Your attachment style may have been shaped by your trauma too. More on attachment styles at the end of this chapter.

Trauma can affect people in many ways. Trauma caused by a caregiver can mean that people seek relationships with those who display similar traits as their caregiver and, therefore, repeat past hurts. Even though this may seem an obvious situation to avoid, it can feel comforting and familiar, even if it is ultimately a negative for the individual concerned.

Selflessness: You may have been brought up with the belief that your purpose in life is to self-sacrifice and put other people's needs before your own. As a result, you may lose a sense of self, of who you really are and want to be. Feelings of guilt and low self-worth are also an issue as you are always on the lookout for everyone else's needs but your own. You may feel that doing anything for yourself is self-indulgent or selfish. Caring for others is everything to you - your self-worth may rely on you caring for others. Therefore, there may be a sense that if you do not get that sense of feeling needed or wanted, by caring for others, you will not be recharging your 'self-worth battery'. Ultimately, it is learning to recharge that self-worth battery ourselves and feeling positive about ourselves without needing the validation of others. This ultimately frees us to help others in a 'boundaried' and healthy way.

Important note: Should you be affected by any of the above, you may wish to get additional professional support to help you heal and process things so that you feel in a happier and stronger place to face the issues that lie within your relationship.

Exercise – Please write down your answer

* In what ways do you feel your upbringing and life events so far have affected your relationship today?

Another important factor in the roles we play in our relationship, is our attachment style.

We will look at the 4 main attachment styles below:

* Secure attachment
* Anxious attachment
* Avoidant attachment
* Disorganised attachment

Let's have a look at them in more detail and see how these attachment styles can affect your relationship.

Secure attachment

A person is able to have a secure attachment style when their parents or caregivers were able to respond to their child's needs throughout their childhood in a consistent, positive and healthy way. As an adult, they are confident and able to form healthy relationships. They are able to support their partners and accept support in return. They can express their emotions in a healthy way.

Anxious attachment

Anxious attachments usually develop when a caregiver or parent is both caring and absent in the child's life. This could be because the caregiver was struggling with issues of their own and was, therefore, unable to always be present. The death of one of the caregivers, or if a parent was working away from home, can all be factors. In adulthood, the person with anxious attachment may feel insecure in a relationship and feel their partner may cheat or leave them. At times, they may end the relationship 'first' in the belief that it is just a matter of time before their partner leaves them.

Avoidant attachment

This style usually develops when a child has been neglected in some way in their childhood. If needs are not met, hope will gradually get replaced by protective barriers against feeling neglected or unwanted in the future. As adults, they tend to become very independent and can cut emotions off easily. As partners, they may be emotionally unavailable and feel that their partner is 'asking too much' of them in the relationship.

Disorganised attachment

Disorganised attachment often develops from having experienced or witnessed abuse, either physical, sexual or mental, to self or to others close to them in childhood. It is the most challenging of the insecure attachment styles. The parent or caregiver who is seen by the child as being responsible for their safety is now also, after having abused that child, seen as unsafe. When the child becomes an adult, they have a need to be loved as well as a need to protect themselves. This can cause a lot of pain and anxiety when wanting a relationship. Lonely without love, they need to feel loved and wanted. But lack of self-worth as well as protecting against hurt means they often sabotage a relationship in fear of being hurt.

Exercise

* Do you recognise any of these styles in yourself? If so, how does it impact your relationship today?

You may wish to show each other what you have written down. This exercise is to gain a deeper understanding of one another, so boundaries may be helpful here. Showing this exercise to each other may make you or your partner feel vulnerable to criticism or negative comments. I would urge you to refrain from commenting negatively about each other's style and impact on the relationship at this stage. Take it as a deeper understanding of one another and the way you both behave in the relationship. And as a result, a step closer to a more profound and meaningful relationship too.

If you identify with some of the issues and feel they impact not only the relationship but you as an individual too, you may wish to work with a qualified therapist to help free yourself of these past hurts.

We will now look at 'triggers' in relationships.

In this context, triggers mean a chain of emotional thoughts and reactions that have been put in motion.

Below are some examples of possible triggers and the emotions and thoughts that may arise from them:

Trigger when a partner is…	Your possible emotion/thought
Spending a lot of time elsewhere	Fear of an affair
Showing your children/pet affection	Feeling unloved
Too tired for intimacy	Hurt and rejected
Ignoring you or putting you down	Worthlessness

The above shows how certain situations can be triggering or 'push your buttons'. This list is by no means exhaustive.

The following is an example of how triggers can affect a relationship. It was inspired by a couple I worked with:

Paula has just made herself a cup of tea.

Steve – 'Oh, did you not make me a cup of tea then? – Passive aggressive tone

Paula – 'I didn't know you wanted one'

Steve – Feeling annoyed and hurt, withdraws. Becomes detached, moody and resentful.

Paula – 'What's the matter with you?'

Steve – 'You know what the matter is'

Paula – 'I wouldn't ask you if I knew' in an elevated voice. Getting irritated.

Steve – 'You are so selfish' then proceeds to list all the times in the last 10 years that he felt Paula
was thoughtless or selfish

Paula – Retaliates and shouts back her grievances over the last ten years

Steve and Paula – At this point, both are shouting and not listening to each other and so the destructive pattern goes on.

The example above is not about the cup of tea, it is about the feelings and thoughts associated with feeling taken for granted and not being adequately considered. For these clients, there were many years of unprocessed resentments which come out whenever they felt overlooked or unappreciated (triggers). So instead of being annoyed just about the tea, the emotions from past hurts also joined the argument.

Exercise

Now, I would like you to look at the 'tea' scenario above. Look at the interactions and reactions and see if you can come up with a more productive way of communicating between Paula and Steve. This may take some thought as I would like you to think about this from both their points of view.

* What did you come up with?
* Was it easy or challenging?
* Do any of the points raised above resonate with you?
* Were you more sympathetic towards Steve or Paula?
  Please give reasons for this
* Can you think of a recent argument that you have had in your relationship that could have been dealt with differently?

Let us have a look at the scenario if dealt with in a different way now

Steve – 'Where is my cup of tea then (term of endearment)?' – Playful tone

Paula – 'Oh sorry, I didn't know you wanted one'

Steve – 'I know it may sound silly but when you just make yourself a cup of tea, I feel forgotten about. I just feel stressed out and I know we both work hard but I don't want us to 'forget' about the two of us in the middle of it all.

Paula – 'You don't think I am supportive?' A bit defensive

Steve – 'You are supportive (gives an example of how Paula is supportive). I just think that we don't think of each other or appreciate each other enough sometimes. I'm just as guilty of this. For example, when I go to the gym without checking if you are ok with the kids.'

Paula – 'I get it, it is just relentless at the moment and I am in survival mode'
(the conversation turns to that of supporting each other more, moving forward)

There is, of course, the opportunity for either party to be defensive and argumentative throughout, but when triggered, you are being made aware that this is an issue for you. When highlighting the issue, it can be helpful to talk with ownership. In other words, 'I feel I need' rather than 'you never'. The problem with starting the conversation with 'You are…' is that your partner's defences will go up as soon as they feel they are being accused of something. They are feeling attacked and so will 'retaliate' with another attack. This will then usually turn the discussion into an argument rather than a healthy discussion.

Exercise

Using the cup of tea example above, think about a time when you were triggered and reacted very strongly to something.

*   Was it appropriate to the situation?
*   Do you feel that you overreacted?

* What situations press your buttons or trigger you?
* Are there certain things that your partner says, or does, that trigger you?
  If so, what are they?
* Did those situations trigger you in the past?
* Are you aware of why these things are triggering for you?
* Is there a common theme?

Now use this newfound awareness to ensure that you both recognise and are reacting in a sensitive way to each other's triggers. If you are aware that a particular way of being, such as shouting, is triggering to your partner, be sensitive to this. If you are someone who is quite moody and needs time alone to process, tell your partner that you are not ignoring them but you need time alone to process everything that has been said or happened. We will cover in more detail the importance of communicating with one another in the chapter on communication.

A common issue that comes up in the practice room is the 'I'll start when you start'. In an ideal world, you would both make the effort together but sometimes, for various reasons, one partner is not yet ready to do so.

But even if one of you starts and communicates in a healthy, positive way, it can be very impacting on the relationship as a whole. People often react to ways of being. Kindness can cultivate kindness. For example, if you smile at someone at the checkout, you are more likely to have a positive interaction with them. The same applies to personal relationships.

Chapter 3

Communication

'Communication and comprehension are the foundations of a healthy relationship'

What is communication?

It is a way of giving and receiving information from one person to another. This can be done in several ways but is mainly done verbally, by phone or text. Body language can also be used.

Good communication is the bedrock of all relationships. It has come up in every session, which highlights just how important it is when working on our relationships. Whether clients come to see me about a gambling habit, an affair or bereavement in the family, communication between the couple is always looked at as it holds the key to moving forward. Negative communication, however, can lead to misunderstandings, mistrust and conflict.

I remember once being told by a couple that their communication was very good as they argued all the time. It may feel as though this is good communication as you are getting your grievances out but unless they are resolved or processed between each other, they will stay as grievances and reappear time after time with each argument. This will then in turn, build more resentments, more defensive barriers and more misunderstandings.

Healthy communication is not about making general conversation. It is about being honest with our partners. Being open and vulnerable to them in a deeper and more meaningful way. In a way that everyday conversations about work or the weather cannot achieve. Communicating with your partner is to connect with your partner. It is trying to understand and empathise with your partner. It is not just trying to get our point of view heard or agreed with.

You **both** need to be heard and understood.

Exercise

In the following exercise, I would like you to look at the statements and ask yourself if they apply to you as a couple. Write down the answers, and give examples of those answers to the following statements:

My partner and I….

* Communicate in a healthy way
* Speak to each other with respect
* Shout instructions to each other
* Are able to talk openly about our feelings and emotions
* Don't talk. It would only start an argument
* Interrupt each other frequently
* Laugh a lot together
* Call each other hurtful names
* Don't listen to each other
* Support each other in what we say
* Put each other down
* Trust each other not to talk to others about things we want to keep private
* Don't share our emotions with one another
* Encourage each other
* Are complimentary towards each other
* Don't talk very much
* Find each other interesting
* Are interested in each other's opinions
* Apologise when we are in the wrong

What do you feel you have learned from doing the exercise above?

Are there some areas of your communication that stand out as needing attention?

What roles do you feel you both play in these areas?

Exercise

I would like you both to choose one of the above statements to work on.

So, for example, if a partner feels their spouse usually shouts when communicating, their homework request to their partner may be for them to become aware of their shouting and see if they can lower their voice when talking.

Or if interrupting is a constant issue, that could be worked on.

The key for this to work is to choose only one statement and for both parties to agree on the work that they will each undertake. Needless to say, choosing two statements as homework for one partner is not the way to go. Choose one each and you will both feel that you are working towards a happier and closer relationship.

What is your communication style?

Not everyone likes to communicate in the same way. For some people, it is important for them to discuss everything there and then so that they can process the disagreement in order to be able to move on. Another person may need to go away and process what has been said in their own time. You can already see with these two communication styles, how challenging it is for that couple to have both needs met at the same time. Other communicating styles include taking action, being tactile or avoidance.

* What is your communication style?
* What is your partner's communication style?

At times, when I have a couple arguing in front of me, I feel more like a translator than a therapist.

Have you ever found that you say something to your partner and they do not understand what you are saying or what you mean? When I see this pattern emerging in the session, I will ask the clients in turn what they heard and then check in with the other partner to see what they actually meant.

Miscommunication can be due to several factors. One example is being on the defensive and, therefore, pre-empting that your partner will be negative in some way. This can lead to a negative opening statement or response. Both of which can lead to arguments.

If you feel you and your partner simply do not seem to understand each other, it is worth looking at the following points to see if any of them resonate with either of you.

Some causes of miscommunication:

* Resentment
* Lack of empathy
* Defensiveness
* Excessive communication
* Lack of communication
* Cultural differences in terms of communicating with others
* Vagueness
* Different upbringings in terms of communication
* Assumptions

Discussing the above may prove to be very helpful in having a better understanding of each other. As previously discussed, there is potential for a lot of miscommunication when looking at your miscommunication!

Agree to discuss this with an aim for better understanding as opposed to fault finding.

Our personal filters

Our personal filters are created from our life experiences, our self-esteem, our genetic make-up and our general influences in life so far.

Let us have a look at these filters in more detail.

Below is an example of how our personal filter or, how we see life and ourselves internally, comes into play in our relationships. Note how these filters can alter the words we hear:

Julie is married to Chris and is concerned about him as he has been particularly quiet today. Chris has always had low self-esteem. He was severely bullied at school and always doubts himself as a result. He struggles to see anything positive about himself.

Chris – Is exhausted from working hard not to disappoint his boss

Julie – Worried about Chris so asks him 'Are you ok?'

Chris – Chris then may process the words in the following way:

Words that were said hearing	Chris's own filter	What he ends up
'Are you ok?'	I'm uselessJulie thinks	I am not coping

Jason has been going out with Matt for a couple of years. Jason was cheated on in a previous relationship and is struggling with trust issues. Matt is friendly, outgoing and sociable.

Matt – 'I have drinks after work with my team to celebrate our new clients. It is the most lucrative deal our team has managed to get so far!'

Jason – Jason then may process the words in the following way:

Words that were said hearing	Jason's own filter	What he ends up
'..drinks after work..'	People cheat on me	Matt is going to cheat on me

Do you now see how your filters play a fundamental part in your communication?

Do you ever jump to a conclusion? Only to find out that it wasn't the case?

We can also 'filter' the words through our own life experiences. For example, your partner may say to you:

'I like that shirt on you' and mean it in a positive way but if you have had negative comments made to you in the past or feel body conscious for example, you may translate it as any one of the following:

* 'It hides my body so that is why they like it therefore they don't like my body.'
* 'They are only being nice as they are after sex'
* 'They are being sarcastic'
* 'They are just saying that because they don't want me to buy new stuff'

As opposed to:

* 'It is so nice to get compliments'
* 'I do think this shirt suits me'

Another example of filtering words with our own life experiences may be if you said to your partner:

'What if we built it this way?' Your partner may then translate it as one of these:

* 'They are so controlling'
* 'They don't think I am capable of building it'
* 'They are just trying to manipulate me as they know I will like this. They will then have leverage to ask for something for themselves.'
* 'They always interfere'
* 'Yes, I hadn't thought of that. It's a good idea'

The examples above illustrate how our filters can shape and distort what is being said.

It would be helpful for you to have a better awareness of how these filters play a part in your relationship.

Now that you have a better understanding and awareness of how communication is affected by your own thoughts and filters, we can look at how to avoid any misunderstandings and arguments.

The key is awareness. Once we are aware of something we can then pause and challenge our immediate response.

Exercise

The following questions need to be taken into consideration after a disagreement and will need some self-reflection. This may be quite challenging to do. But they will enlighten you as to why and how you argue. It will, therefore, enable any changes that may need to take place in order to have a healthy style of communication.

* Is your response to your partner's words more to do with you and your life experiences or is it more to do with the delivery of their words based on their life experiences?
* Are you particularly sensitive about a subject matter?
* Is your partner particularly sensitive about a subject matter?
* Do you both take these things into consideration when you talk to each other?
* An individual's vulnerable or triggering spot can be considered and dealt with in a sensitive way or it can be used against them as a weapon in communication. Does this resonate with you or your partner?

There are many aspects to positive and healthy communication between a couple.

It is not just the words that you use which are important, the tone is also key. Imagine these words said in the following tones:

'You look great'

* With warmth and a smile
* In a monotonous tone and not having looked at you once
* In a sarcastic way with a smirk
* With impatience and a brusque way of being

Three small words… and yet such a different meaning depending on the tone, as well as the actions that go with it.

Here is another example to show you how tone can affect communication.

Imagine the words said in the following tones:

'I don't think you should do that'

* In a low and threatening tone
* In a caring and warm way
* Playful tone with a smile

The most challenging one to look at is the passive aggressive tone. The 'I didn't mean it like that, YOU are taking it the wrong way', when their tone clearly delivered the words in a negative way. It then becomes like sand in the hand. Your word against theirs. Passive aggressive behaviour usually happens when a person feels resentful or angry but is not able to express it directly to the person concerned. Instead, they will channel that anger or resentment in indirect ways. This is very toxic for both partners.

Let us have a look at an example of this:

Jane had an affair. She doesn't like to be reminded of this, as it makes her feel guilty and have anger towards herself. In this example, she deflects these feelings from her wrongdoings to Kylie, her partner, by using a passive aggressive tone and way of being, as shown below:

Jane – Jane is aware that she stayed out later than she said she would but feels Kylie should be getting over the affair by now and therefore not feel insecure.

Kylie – Is feeling angry that Jane stayed out later than she said she would last night. She feels she has broken her promise to try to repair the relationship after her affair.

Kylie – 'What time did you come home last night?'

Jane – 'You always do this. You are not helping the situation by overreacting all the time. You know your anxiety makes you paranoid' said in what would seem to be a warm and caring tone.

Jane's words and tone may come across to Kylie as caring for the relationship and being concerned about her reaction. What is happening is that she is not taking ownership for her part in the recovery process of their relationship after her affair. But instead, is transferring her guilt and anger unto Kylie by blaming Kylie's alleged 'anxiety and paranoia'.

All too often in sessions, I hear clients using the tone of their voice as weapons against each other.

* Are you aware of the tone that you use when you communicate with your partner?

Another aspect of our voice, when talking to our partner, is volume and pitch.

* Do you or your partner shout or even scream at one another?

Our need to shout and scream comes from our instinct to survive and this is an appropriate response when our lives are under threat. The problem is that when you use it in everyday situations, you become desensitised to the fact that this behaviour can negatively impact a relationship. If you have been brought up in a household where shouting was commonplace, it can also desensitise you regarding its impact in a relationship.

Shouting = A defensive response

When one of you screams or shouts, the other partner may feel attacked so may go into defensive mode. This can either be fighting back (more screaming) or withdrawing into 'safety'. Neither response is conducive to solving or resolving the issue at hand.

Want to stop shouting and screaming at each other? Look at the following question.

* Would you shout and scream at your child's Headteacher, cashier at the till, Doctor or a 5-year-old playing in a park?

I often ask my clients if they would shout and scream at me in the way that they do with one another. Most of the time, I see a look of horror on their face and I have not come across any who have said that they would. The main reason given is that they respect me and, therefore, would never do that. So, I challenge them, by highlighting that they respect me (a professional, granted) but someone they barely know or care about. And yet they do not respect the person they love and have decided to share their life with enough not to shout at them. This is worth thinking about. They would treat their therapist better than their partner!

Name calling

I also use this 'formula' when looking at the words said within a relationship. I am still saddened by the words used between two people who have chosen to be together. When I see that this is an issue in the relationship, I ask each client to write down the names that they have been called by their partner. B*tch, fat sl*g, c**t, stupid and thick are just a few of the words that are used to describe the one they fell in love with. These words leave scars, so it is even more challenging to heal from them. Once they have written down the words, I ask them to swap their 'list' and then read it silently in their head. Shame and disbelief are frequent emotions that arise from this exercise. I then ask the same question as I do about shouting. Would they call me a fat sl*g or a b*tch?

This is a real eye opener for most couples and there is a mental seed that is planted from that moment on of how devastating words can be, and that what is said in a moment of anger can have a lasting impact and create deep wounds.

After years of arguing, couples can develop 'defensive responses'. They are on the defensive before the other person has even opened their mouths, making it less likely that their partner will be heard 'neutrally'. For example, if put-downs have been part of the relationship, **every** sigh, comment or gesture will be seen as a put-down.

Awareness of how you respond to your partner is key. Try to practice pausing for a moment before responding to your partner. It will give you an opportunity to think about what you are hearing. If you are working on this book together, you may wish to highlight to your partner what you thought you heard and ask them to clarify if this was accurate. If not, what did they actually mean?

If you still feel that your partner is putting you down, then this needs to be looked at and discussed, as this will eventually erode a relationship.

If something that is said triggers you, highlight this at the time. Understanding these triggers and the reason why you have them, whether from a childhood trauma, a toxic past relationship or any other impacting event, and sharing this with your partner, can create a better understanding and more empathy for one another. This would have to be discussed beforehand in order to avoid falling into old habits and starting another argument when you are trying to work on your communication instead!

Some couples withdraw from one another instead of saying what is bothering them. This can then fester and result in having built-up resentment. There can also be a feeling that a partner 'should' be able to read their mind. This is one of the biggest problems that I come across in my practice. A lack of communication coupled with the expectation that their partner will read their mind. The lack of response (at times due to not being able to read their mind) can then be translated as being unresponsive, ignoring them or being uncaring. When something is not said, the other person will fill in the gaps for themselves. This is not always accurate. The gap has now been filled with what you think is wrong and so now becomes **your** truth and you now see it as a fact.

Here is an example of how this looks in everyday life:

Rebecca – Had some bad news at work. Since coming home, she has been quiet and has not smiled much

Robert – Having asked her what is wrong and not got very much feedback, he then fills in the gap with thoughts that she must be in a mood with him

* Have you ever found yourself expecting your partner to read your mind and 'just know' what you want or what you are thinking?
* Do you ever 'fill in the gaps' and presume that they must be thinking this way or that way and it then becomes a fact in your mind?

Now that you have this awareness, bring that awareness into how you communicate. Have the knowledge that your partner cannot always know what is on your mind unless you communicate this to them and vice versa. Try to refrain from 'filling in the gaps' with your own thoughts. If you both communicate more, there should be less unknowns, less guessing or presumptions about what each other is thinking, resulting in fewer misunderstandings.

Listening

'I'll listen to you when you listen to me'

When I was studying to be a therapist, I remember thinking that they spent an inordinate amount of time talking about and practising listening. I had always thought this was a natural way of being for everyone. We do this on an everyday basis, so why spend so long studying it?

It was not until I put my listening skills into practice with my peers that I realised the difference between listening and LISTENING. I realised that, at times, I would pre-empt my colleagues' responses. I would also be more attentive to some aspects of what is being said than to others. In my enthusiasm (to help), I would, at times, interrupt my colleagues and, as a result, invalidate their words in the process.

Exercise

The following exercise will help you to think about your listening skills in your relationship. If working on this as a couple, please write down your answers individually:

* When your partner is talking, do you really listen to what is being said?
* Do you interrupt frequently?
* Do you switch off 'knowing what the other is going to say'?
* Do you put thought into choosing a time and place when talking to each other about important or emotive subjects, so that you are able to listen?

* Do you reflect or take action on what you have heard?
* When you respond to each other – is it in the way YOU would like to be responded to or what your PARTNER needs?

Here are some ways to improve your listening skills and, therefore, improve communication between both of you:

* If possible, make eye contact during a conversation or when asking a question. A lot of couples shout to each other from one room to the next whilst doing other things.
* If you would like your partner to listen to you on a matter that could cause emotional upset or an argument, think about the time and place for such a discussion.
* For both of you, decide to make more of an effort not to interrupt each other. When we interrupt, we are sending messages to the other person implying that what they are saying is not important or valid. They then may feel that **they** are not important or valid as a consequence.
* Be aware of each other's communication styles. Listen to your partner when they say they need to think about it. If you need to talk about it all now, you may wish to set a time frame so that you both reconvene in half an hour for example, so that you both compromise and, therefore, both feel heard.
* I sometimes pause a session and ask a client what they heard their partner say. Then, I will ask the partner who was talking to clarify what they meant. At times, this can vary greatly. You may also want to pause at times and ask each other how they interpreted your words and vice versa. This way, you will sort out any potential misunderstandings before they arise.

When communication has broken down completely, some of the exercises in this chapter may seem too difficult at first. If this is the case, start by writing (factual and positive only) notes to each other in order to start the communication process. This will then build on the positive without the possibility of every interaction turning into an argument. Maybe write thank you notes to start with. 'Thank you for emptying the dishwasher… for coming with me to the doctor's…'

Once a healthier communication foundation has been achieved, go back over this chapter with your partner and work through the exercises at your own pace in order to build on that foundation.

Words are very impactful … they can be weapons that can leave deep scars or be powerful shields that heal, empower and protect.

Chapter 4

What's the problem?

'When people have strong internal defence systems, they are very efficient at keeping hurt out.
And love too'

Now that we have looked at communication, we can start exploring the issues and problems within your relationship.

It is important to understand how you arrived at where you are today and the reasons behind this. Most couples I work with will be able to talk about arguments they have had or things they do not like about each other but do not know where the 'nucleus or centre points' of the problems lie. To create a new and better way forward, you need to understand the road you have just travelled. This will help you to avoid making the same negative or toxic decisions and ensure you make the right decisions for the both of you in the future.

* Have you been neglecting each other along the way?
* Or neglecting yourself?
* Is your partner neglecting you?
* Has resentment built up for one or both of you?
* Has your partnership been affected by an affair or break of trust?
* Has communication broken down?

Part of the reason that counselling can be challenging is that it is key for both parties to recognise and understand their role in the troubles they are experiencing. What you each contribute to the relationship in both a positive and negative way. Couples who come to see me tend to look at their relationship from their own, individual, point of view. This point of view may be affected by stresses in life, depression, or anxiety for example.

It takes courage to look at ourselves and be able to see, challenge and admit our part in problems within the couple but this is key to the healing of our relationships.

Exercise

Use the exercise below to gain a better understanding of where the problems lie and how much they affect you both as a couple.

Do you both have similar views on:

* Finances
  Agree   Disagree

* Parenting
  Agree   Disagree

* The running of your home
  Agree   Disagree

* Time as a couple
  Agree   Disagree

* Work
  Agree   Disagree

* Trust
  Agree   Disagree

* Infidelity
  Agree   Disagree

* Relationship priorities
  Agree   Disagree

* Respect
  Agree   Disagree

* Pornography
  Agree   Disagree

* Jealousy
  Agree   Disagree

Before we continue, I would like you to look at the points above that you agreed with. Now, ask yourself the following:

Do I agree because….

1. It means a quiet life
2. I am not able to disagree (please give reasons for this)
3. My partner has always made the decisions
4. I feel happy with the decisions
5. The choices we make work well for us as a couple

If you answered 1,2 or 3 you may wish to look at your role in the relationship. If you feel that the decisions and choices do not include your wants and needs, go back over this exercise and do it again with your needs in mind.

Where do you disagree?

For ease of reference, we will look at each issue separately.

Finances

It may not come as a surprise to you that this is a frequent topic that comes up in sessions.
Money.
What does it represent for you?
What does it represent for your partner?

Is it freedom of choice, power, success, control, fun…? Financial disagreements are often based on the effects that having or not having money has on us as individuals and our lives.

Exercise

Please look at the statements below and state whether you agree or disagree:

* Money is a means to an end
  Agree   Disagree

* Money gives me power in the relationship
  Agree   Disagree

* Money gives me control
  Agree   Disagree

* Money is there to have fun with
  Agree   Disagree

* Money gives me freedom
  Agree   Disagree

* Lack of money makes me feel vulnerable
  Agree   Disagree

* Lack of money is freeing
  Agree   Disagree

* Lack of money is stressful
  Agree   Disagree

* Lack of money means less power in the relationship
  Agree   Disagree

Having completed the exercise, were there any surprises as to how you both view money? If so, what were they?

These questions can be very enlightening. They can help you to understand what role money plays in your relationship and how much of an impact it is having, Negatively or positively.

Now that you have a basic knowledge of how finances affect your relationship, let us explore this in more detail:

* Are you both aware of your current financial situation?
* Do you both have your own personal 'guilt free' money to spend on whatever you like without having to ask your partner?'

* If not, is this something that would help to alleviate some of your financial resentment?

* Are you both happy with the way your finances are run?
* Do you have individual accounts? Joint account? Or joint with additional individual accounts?
* Is this working for you both? If not, what would be a better option?
* Does your individual spend feel fair and equal when taking into account the money coming in? If not, does this bring up resentment?
* What are your spending styles? Is one of you thrifty and the other a big spender?
* How do your spending habits affect the relationship?
* Are either of you in debt? If yes, is this causing issues between you?

Every couple's situation is unique but if finances are causing problems between you, here are some ways of dealing with these problems that clients have said were beneficial to them.

* Creating either a joint bank account or individual accounts to cover the monthly bills and each taking out a set amount as 'Freedom Money'. In other words, guilt free money. This can help where one partner is working in a paid job and the child carer or homemaker feels they have to ask whenever they need or want to purchase anything.
* If one of you has a spending habit, an addiction, or a gambling habit, it may be helpful for the other partner to look after the finances whilst they get professional help in order to be able to overcome their addiction. Hoping someone is going to change is not enough. If your finances have been severely impacted by the habit or addiction, it is for your partner to prove that they have overcome it over a certain period of time. This will also allow trust to be rebuilt. And only then, when the trust has been rebuilt can you both run the finances on an equal footing.
* You may find it helpful to have transparency with regards to finances. This is especially important when a partner has had an addiction or has issues with spending money. 'Going through' the

finances together every so often can also help in these situations. This can also help partners who feel they have had the finances 'dumped' on them. Even if finances are not your forte, it is important to be supportive of each other. This could simply mean having the knowledge of how much it costs to run the home without dealing with the finances on a day-to-day basis.

* When one partner earns more than the other, it can feel very disempowering, especially if constantly highlighted by the main wage earner. Relationships, jobs, situations are not static. Life evolves and changes. So too can the incomes within a relationship. The important focus here is on what you both bring to the relationship as a whole. Earning a six-figure salary in itself does not mean a happier relationship. Money can ease worries or make our lives more comfortable but it is how we connect with one another that is key to a happy relationship and this has no monetary value.

It is important to appreciate and value what each of you brings to the table. If your partner works long hours in a stressful job or with a difficult commute, let them know you appreciate what they do and that you empathise with the challenges they face. The same applies to an at home parent for example. Appreciate that they may feel on call 24/7 and may not have had the breaks in the day that an outside job allows, and in turn, empathise with the challenges that they face. When we feel heard, understood, and appreciated, money becomes less of an issue and is less likely to be used as a weapon because you are a team and each of you play an important part within that team.

Parenting

Whether you have grown up children, young children, have become a stepparent or a primary carer for a child and are blending two families together, how you want to raise your children is often an emotive subject for couples. If parenting is causing a lot of conflicts, you will need to look at where the issues lie.

The following exercise will help to clarify where the issues are between both of you when it comes to parenting. It is very important to write these answers down as opposed to saying them out loud. Being a very emotive subject, there can be a concern that emotions will cloud and take over in this exercise.

Exercise

Try to look at things from a more matter of fact way when answering the following questions:

* Do you agree on some of the parenting?
* If so, what do you agree on?
* What do you disagree on?
* If you disagree on some issues, what are those issues?
* What are the three most important aspects of your child's upbringing?
* Are these aspects non-negotiable or is there room for compromise?

For some couples I have worked with, as soon as they have a child, they, as individuals, adopt a strong belief in how their child should be brought up. This belief tends to cement itself as being the right way of doing things. This can make it difficult for the other partner to feel included or that 'they are doing it right'. And yet children will learn from both of you. You can both bring positive aspects to your child's life.

Using the answers to the exercise above, look at the three most important aspects of your child's upbringing. Now, look at those aspects and try to be as specific as possible. For example, if it is happiness, what does that look like? Freedom in certain areas, more attention, encouragement? Or if it is discipline, what areas of the child's discipline are important to you? To respect other people, to say please and thank you, to tidy up after themselves?

Now look at each other's list – are they totally different, the same or a mixture of the two?

Once you have the information, it is important that you both understand what the reasons are behind your answers. For example, if you wrote home-schooling is important, highlight the reasons why this is important to you. You may have been home-schooled yourself and had a very enriching education and childhood as a result. Your partner may have concerns on this, and it is important that you also hear their point of view. They may have concerns over the lack of social contact with other children their age. It is about communicating your thoughts and the reasoning behind your thoughts on parenting rather than it being a statement that this is 'the right way' and how it is going to be.

Maybe you had a great childhood and want your child to benefit from some of the positive experiences you had. Or you were bullied at school or had an unhappy childhood and that influences your thoughts on parenting. You may have had a very relaxed childhood with few boundaries or a very strict one where there was very little freedom. You may have been raised in a blended family, with both biological parents present, in foster care or in a single parent household. These all impact our choices and decisions for our own children.

The key to resolving parental conflicts is firstly to be willing to listen to your partner's thoughts on why something is important to them. Like a lot of our actions, it is the emotion behind our beliefs that drives them. Be empathic to each other's emotions with regards to your child. With a better understanding, you can then look at ways of incorporating both of your thoughts and beliefs. Your child's upbringing may be richer and more fulfilled as a result.

Blended families can raise additional issues to the ones mentioned above. One of the most common problems that I hear about in my practice is that of stepparents or stepchildren not getting on. This can be particularly difficult if everyone is living under the same roof. The biological parent of the child can often become the referee between their child and their partner. This usually means that one party will be left feeling hard done by.

Either party can feel that the other is given preferential treatment, more attention or time than the other. This can make for a very stressful and toxic dynamic where neither the parent, stepparent or child are happy. So, what does that mean for your relationship? For your relationship to survive this dynamic, it is important to ensure that healthy, appropriate boundaries and actions are put in place.

Exercise

Doing the following exercise will help you to look at the actions and boundaries within your family dynamic:

* Do you spend time alone with your children on a regular basis?
* Do you spend time alone with your partner on a regular basis?
* Do you feel guilty that you are not meeting everybody's needs at any one time?
* Do you feel disrespected by:
  Your partner?
  Your children?
  Your stepchildren?
* If yes, please give examples

Have a look at your answers. It is important for each of you to have a better understanding of what it is like and what difficulties you each face. This can then help to have a constructive and positive conversation about how you can support each other and the child or children involved, resulting in a happier blended family life.

If you do not work together in blending a family, you may end up feeling resentful and lonely and all the relationships within your blended family will suffer as a result. The first thing that needs to happen is communication. If you are struggling with this, go back to the chapter on communication and work through that first before continuing with this book.

Once you feel you are able to communicate better, look at what is important to both of you. If it is respect, for example, put boundaries in place to ensure that even if all parties are not the best of friends, mutual respect is required by all parties concerned. This means the adults as well as the children.

Hoping that things will change by themselves and that people will get on is not an effective way to change a situation. Look at the situation, talk about it to your partner and work together to find a way forward.

You may not be looking at a perfect scenario, but a good enough one instead. More importantly, you can then build from this and work together to have more harmony in your household.

The running of your home

A lot of my clients are surprised at just how much resentment and anger are related to everyday chores of running a home. Things we may have been happy to do at the beginning of the relationship may now be cause for resentment. Increased working hours, stresses, having a family, these all change how much time and energy we have. If we feel we are always taking on the lion's share, we may feel unappreciated, taken for granted and undervalued. This can lead to a change in dynamics between partners.

If you find yourself constantly asking your partner to pick up after themselves or do their fair share of work, it can make you feel like a parent talking to their child. Your partner, in turn, can feel as though they are treated as a child too.

There can be an added element to the running of your home. Standards. One person's standards may mean an immaculate home whilst the other has more of a relaxed attitude when it comes to housework.

What is important to you as an individual when it comes to your home?

This may seem a trivial question but if you both have different ideas on what is important, then a conversation resulting in compromise needs to be had.

The homework I give couples who struggle with division of the housework is to write a list. A chore list. This may sound forced and not very romantic but the results you get from putting the list into practice has shown itself to earn more loving, more respect and more appreciation.
I also find that, after a short while, the chore list is no longer needed as it becomes second nature. Both partners are able to see the benefits in helping each other out when it comes to running their home.

How to agree on what is on that list in the first place can be challenging, which is one of the reasons we tend to map it all out in the session. The reasons for the difficulties, often show up as a lack of time, energy, work and looking after children.

Unless one of you is solely responsible for the running of the house with no other jobs or responsibilities such as looking after children, or being a carer to a family member, then you are both on an equal footing in terms of the division of labour. It is helpful for both of you to discuss and look at what time you can both contribute towards the running of your home.

It is important for both of you to show appreciation for each other's part in helping out. 'Just because they always do it' is not an excuse for lack of appreciation. You are creating a life and home together and how you live that life and run your home is fundamental to your life as a couple. After all, for most of us, it is where we spend the majority of our time together.

Couple time

How much time do you spend together as a couple?

When I say 'as a couple', I am referring to relaxed, enjoyable time together (just the two of you – not with family, friends or children) when you can reconnect with each other.

Sitting on opposite ends of the sofa in the same room, not talking, whilst watching TV and being on your phones does not constitute 'couple time'. It is better to reconnect with your partner for ten minutes a day over a cup of tea or a glass of wine than to have a date night once a month. Relationships need nurturing. People need to feel that they matter, that they are loved and cared for. A daily connection keeps these feelings alive.

Time is a real issue for many couples. Once you have accomplished all that you have to do in your daily life, exhaustion can set in. This can result in 'couple time' feeling like another thing to add to the 'to do list'. It is because of this, that your own individual free time will be looked at first in a session, before looking at 'couple time'. Once some individual time has been put in place, clients say that they have more energy as well as feel more relaxed. Chapter 6 covers self-care and individual time in more depth.

Lack of time can build resentment in a relationship. I call resentment 'the silent killer'. I call it 'silent' as it tends not to be voiced. When we feel resentful, we tend to show this through anger, hurtful words or internalise our emotions and go quiet. The silent part is that we do not necessarily address what we are feeling resentful about. The problem with resentment is that, unless it is processed and dealt with, it will erode and chip away at the relationship. If you find that it is an issue in your relationship, use the tools you have learned in Chapter 3 on communication to process resentments as they arise.

Exercise

The following exercise will help you both in understanding what your needs are and with this information, plan time for you as a couple:

* Are you able to relax with your partner?
* If not, what needs to be addressed so that you can relax in their company?
* Do you prefer to go out as a couple alone or as a couple with a group of friends?
* Do you feel your partner prefers to go out as a couple alone or as a couple with a group of friends?
* Ideally, how would you want to spend your 'couple time' together?
* How do you feel your partner would want to spend your 'couple time' together?
* How did you use to spend your time together when you first met?
* Do you miss those times?
* If yes, can these times still be lived (albeit with some compromises or changes)?
* Realistically, how much time can you ring-fence for you as a couple each week?

It is not enough just to have this information. You need to talk about your time together. What ideas do you both have on outings and how the time could be spent? Writing it down in your calendar or diary may seem unromantic but it then becomes as much of a priority as a doctor's appointment instead of getting forgotten and falling by the wayside. And that would be unromantic!

Work

Whether you are working away from home, are self-employed, or your work is based at home, your working conditions can have a direct impact on your relationship. Any changes in your work situation can also have a big impact.

For most of us, work takes up a large proportion of our time and energy. The issues start when we are looking at the remaining time (and energy) we have left. If your week were to be divided in a pie chart, how much of your week do you devote to the following?

*   Work
*   Self
*   Partner
*   Children
*   Family
*   Friends
*   Running of the home

Exercise

Each draw your own pie chart and include the relevant topics such as working, leaving out the children section if you do not have children.

* What does your pie chart look like?
* What does your partner's pie chart look like?
* Are they similar or completely different?

Doing this exercise is a good way to have a better awareness of how you spend your time. It also helps to reflect on this exercise and to look at the changes that need to be made in order to have a more balanced way of living.

A frequent issue raised is when one partner is working outside of the home whilst the other is looking after the children. When the end of the day arrives, they both want and need to relax. They both need a break from having worked all day. If this is not looked at and each of their needs are not met, resentment can build up and slowly erode the relationship.

So, going back to the issue, what can be done when both of you need a break? Most of the time, there is no one else there to be able to look after the children so that you can both take a break.

Firstly, acknowledge the facts. You have both been working all day, you are both tired, you have both faced challenges and you both deserve a break. This is where a lot of couples compete with one another. 'My partner has…more time, less stress, loves what they do, has a restful commute, is able to relax when the children are asleep…'. These are just some of the reasons given to me as to why they should have the break instead of their partner when they get home.

Everything is relative but life is not static. Even if your partner loves their job or being a parent for example, they still need a break and so do you.

The solutions lie in working with 'what is'. If you only have each other to turn to for support, work together on this. Support each other. In a session, we would look at what this means in practical terms. It would be difficult to give you a 'one size fits all' answer as everybody's schedule and lifestyles are so different, but the following example may help:

Partner 1 – Comes home. Has half an hour wind down whilst partner 2 looks after the children

Partner 2 – Then has half an hour wind down whilst partner 1 looks after the children

Partner 1 and 2 – They would then jointly cook, bathe the children, and put them to bed

Partner 1 and 2 – They would then have some time together

The above may seem obvious, but life has a habit of taking over and we just go into survival mode in these situations. It is only when we sit down and look at how we are running our lives (or how it is running us) that we have more clarity on it.

The key in the example above, is that each partner would need to look after the children for the half an hour when it is the other partner's turn to switch off. If you feel you cannot relax or switch off in that time because you are still in the house, then going for a walk or a drive may help.

The formula above can be applied to so many aspects of your relationship.

Give each other a break – literally!

Trust

How important is trust in your relationship?

You may both have a different perspective on what constitutes being trustworthy. Each individual has their own boundaries that they base their trust on. What one person feels is breaking the trust, another may be completely comfortable with. Such as kissing someone else for example.

To discover what your individual boundaries are when it comes to trust, answer the following:

*	I trust my partner when talking to others	Yes
		No
*	I trust my partner in having friends of the opposite sex or same sex depending on sexual orientation	Yes
		No

*	We both agree on what constitutes infidelity	Yes
		No
*	If trust is broken, it will end the relationship	Yes
		No
*	Broken trust can be rebuilt	Yes
		No
*	I am trustworthy	Yes
		No
*	I trust my partner	Yes
		No
*	I take my partner for granted	Yes
		No

To trust someone is to believe that they will honour you as a person and safeguard your relationship. In other words, protect rather than harm the relationship. When someone breaks the trust, it is rarely done with the intent to hurt. But it does hurt. Breaking your partner's trust means that you will need to work to rebuild that trust. For the partner whose trust has been broken, you have a choice of giving your partner the opportunity of repairing the relationship or you may choose to move on with your life.

Some may feel they do not have that choice. This may be due to financial reasons, for example. If you are not earning and are the primary carer for the children, you may feel that you cannot just up and leave should you wish to do so. In this and any other situation where the trust has been broken, I would highlight the need to look at your lives overall and envisage what lays ahead if no changes are made.

If you feel you can work on your relationship, then the repair work and healing process would need to be looked at. If, however, you feel that the trust keeps on being broken and the relationship is a toxic one, you may want to take steps to end the relationship. This may mean having financial independence for yourself or ensure you have the right support throughout the process of leaving that relationship.

You want to give your relationship another chance. What is the next step?

One of the first things that I highlight when working with broken trust is the need for actions rather than words. By the time they have sat down in my practice room, the apologies would have been made, and the 'I'll never do it again' has been said over and over. They have dissected the break of trust and they are now wondering what to do with all the heightened emotions flying around their body and mind.

Over the course of the weekly sessions, I will give them homework to start rebuilding the trust. Here are some examples you can both work on if you are wanting to rebuild the trust in your relationship:

* Total transparency for a set period of time. No passwords on any devices, social platforms etc. If a partner is feeling insecure because of an affair, they need to be able to ask the other to see their phone. Showing them the phone is an action. This is tangible and can help with the rebuilding of trust. **But,** this is only healthy for a set period of time. You would not want to still be asking to see your partner's phone a year or two years on, as that would indicate that the relationship is not in a healthy place. It would also not be healthy to look at your partner's devices behind their back.

* What action can the offending partner take to rebuild trust?
  If they have broken trust through gambling or drugs, they could show their commitment by seeking therapy and having total transparency with the bank accounts.
  If the break of trust is due to an affair, they could change gyms, routines or job to ensure that they are not in direct contact with the person they had an affair with. This is not always possible, so other ways of rebuilding the trust would need to take place. If they work in a gym, for example, they may be able to change shifts with a colleague.

* I ask each partner to think of what they would need from their partner to rebuild the trust. An example would be for one partner to say: 'I need you to come home when you finish work, rather than have drinks with your work colleagues. As the affair was with a work colleague, it makes me feel insecure at the moment'. The other partner's need may be 'I need you to see that I am trying to do the repair work'.

* The repairing of trust can be done by showing that you care and are committed to your partner. Helping them out more., listening to what they are saying and taking actions that show you have heard and taken on board what was said.

To do this at home, ask your partner what **one** thing you could do that would help. Then your partner needs to ask what **one** thing they could do to help the healing process. Less is more on this. You may want to put all the work in from the off to speed up the process, but this is counterproductive. It is better to do one action consistently for a longer period than do 10 things for a couple of weeks and then stop doing them altogether. When the homework is being done consistently, it shows a desire to make the effort. A willingness to rebuild trust.

Rebuilding trust is a choice. If you feel your partner is truly repentant and is unlikely to break your trust in this way again, you would both need to move on from the past. If it is going to be brought up in every argument, then the relationship will eventually be eroded. The partner who has broken the trust may feel like no matter what they do, it will never be enough, and the relationship may be impacted as a result. There needs to be a point in time when you make the decision to trust them or you decide that they cannot be trusted.

Infidelity

I am often asked whether a relationship can survive an affair and my answer is always the same. If both partners are willing and able to work at the relationship, it can survive and even become stronger as a result of the work and journey taken. If, however, your partner has cheated on you repeatedly, no amount of work that you do as an individual will stop this. They need to seek professional help to enable them to discover the reasons behind their behaviour.

When I talk of the work involved, I am referring to the repair work that is needed from the person who has broken the trust. Trust has been explored in more detail in the previous section. The partner who has been betrayed will need to heal and process what has happened. Both will then need to look at the relationship as a whole. An affair is never the answer to any problem but having a better understanding of how it came into your lives is a necessary part of the process to ensure that it does not happen again in the future.

To rebuild the relationship, it is helpful to look at what ingredients are needed for the repair and healing to take place:

* Trust needs to be rebuilt
* Trust needs to be earned
* Words are no longer as effective with trust. Actions are needed
* There needs to be a point in time when you decide whether you choose to trust your partner or not
* Transparency will be needed for a period of time to rebuild the trust
* It is key to look at how the affair came about, not just look at its impact after the discovery

There are, at times, additional issues that may complicate the healing process. One example of this would be if the third-party contacts the partner who had the affair. The partner who cheated does not want to cause more trouble so does not say anything. The hurt partner finds out. As a result rebuilding the trust is now more fragile than it was before. As with the other examples when trust has been broken, total transparency and communication are needed.

The fear is that they may feel awkward or cause an argument. Clients say that they would far rather be told of the contact and that they would trust their partner more rather than less. Worth noting.

I have discovered a pattern emerging in couples who are recovering from an affair. When the repair work is being done and the trust is being rebuilt, there can be a sense of 'rebirth' for the relationship. Some say it is like a 'honeymoon period'. This is usually the result of having nearly lost a loved one and having done a lot of the reparatory work which brings couples closer and makes the relationship stronger. It is worth noting that, like honeymoons, the level of emotions and feelings can become less heightened over time and this does not mean that you are going backwards in your recovery. If the work has been put in place, you will still be left with a stronger relationship and sense of closeness, but heightened emotions cannot be sustained over long periods of time.

I often set up a check-in with couples who are recovering from an affair. This check-in is usually a month or so after our last session. It is during these sessions that clients often become aware that some of the old habits have crept back into their relationship. Life stresses, busy lives and at times complacency can sometimes interfere with the times you were spending together as a couple. Clients can sometimes fall into the trap that 'they don't need to bother doing this or that anymore because they are ok now'. Relationships are like plants. Feed them or they will eventually get sick and die.

Once you have done the repair work and feel you are in a good place, make a note in your diary, for a month ahead to review how you are both doing. I find that just having the date in place to talk about your relationship can make a big difference. It is akin to having a health check-up.

Relationship priorities

I have worked with couples who differ on what is the most important thing to them in a relationship. For one partner, it may be to accept their family, parents and siblings, as they are an integral part of their life. Whereas for the other partner, time as a couple was the most important part of a relationship. So, what is the answer? Compromises. Or gifts, as I prefer to call them.

When working with couples, the idea of compromising can be received quite negatively. Almost as though they have weakened or given in, but the truth is that we compromise daily without giving it a second thought. Your local shop does not have the brand of coffee you like but you have no coffee left, you compromise and buy another brand. Meeting a friend, but you both live quite far away from each other so you compromise and meet halfway. You normally end your day at 6pm, but the person you need to meet up with can only see you at 7pm. Another compromise.

* How often do you feel you compromise in your relationship?
* How often do you feel your partner compromises in your relationship?

It is about honouring what is important to you as well as what is important to your partner. Whenever couples highlight what is important to them as individuals, it can, at times, feel as though their thoughts and ideas are more important, more valid, and 'right' and that their partner's thoughts and ideas are 'wrong'. Unless we are looking at hurtful or abusive beliefs, then what is to say that one person's belief or priority is right and the other is wrong? Could it be more to do with ways of being, the way we have been brought up and our experiences in life? This is quite challenging to think about, but it is a crucial part in looking at the differences within your relationship in a healthier, more positive way.

In finding compromises, you are both acknowledging your partner's needs.

Couples' priorities can differ when it comes to how their leisure and fun time is spent. One of you may prefer to socialise with friends whilst the other may prefer to spend time as a couple instead. We are all different in our needs, likes and dislikes. If your needs are met as an individual as well as within the couple, you will have a good foundation for your life and relationship. You cannot be happy as a couple if you are sacrificing all your needs, hopes and wants for the other.

What gift or compromise could you both give each other when it comes to each other's priorities, wants and needs in the relationship?

Respect

Do you respect yourself? Do you respect and have appropriate boundaries for yourself? A relationship is not a couple joined at the hip with one set of boundaries. A relationship is made up of two individuals. How can we hope to have respect for our partner if we do not have respect for ourselves?

How would you feel if your partner called you names? Would you accept it, tolerate it or is it unacceptable to you? Now ask yourself the same question but change your partner to a close friend or relative. Would you tolerate it less, more or the same? If you feel differently, can you think of reasons behind this? Now, ponder on this. Do you put yourself down and call yourself names in your head?

If communication is the cornerstone of relationships, then respect is the foundation. How we communicate, interact and think of ourselves and our partners are a mirror as to how much respect is in place.

How can we identify respect in a relationship?

* Partners will listen to each other
* Both points of view will be acknowledged even if not agreed with
* They will not resort to put downs, name calling or gaslighting
* Each partner is willing to compromise
* There is consideration regarding the impact of any decisions made on the other partner
* There is respect for each other's moral code and set of boundaries

How can we identify disrespect in a relationship?

* Taking each other for granted
* Using a partner's insecurity against them
* Passive aggressive behaviours
* Not listening to your partner
* Calling your partner names
* Ignoring your partner
* Belittling your partner
* Not willing to compromise

If you find that you are struggling to show respect to yourself, you may find it helpful to either read more on this subject or seek outside support so that you can respect yourself in the way you deserve. It will then be easier to look at the respect in your relationship.

Pornography

Pornography is an issue if both partners are not in agreement with it. Some of my clients have described it as the third element in their relationship and some as an enjoyable addition to their sex life. The issues start when one partner watches porn as a means to 'escape' from their life or as a way to avoid intimacy with their partner. Watching porn secretly on your own as opposed to both partners choosing to watch it together generally has a negative impact on relationships. There is less intimacy, less commitment to the sexual side of the relationship.

There can also be blurred lines between the scenes or acts in pornography and real life. The partner who watches porn alone may want the couple's sex life to be based on the pornographic images and scenes. This can cause the other partner a lot of distress and a feeling of falling short of what is, essentially, an unrealistic setup and constructed image or scene.

How the individuals within the couple feel about pornography impacts how pornography will be viewed in a relationship. For some, it feels like a betrayal, a break of trust whilst their partner may see it as harmless fun. Secrecy surrounding porn can really affect the trust element in the relationship too.

If you are not of the same opinion regarding pornography or if pornography is causing issues within your relationship in the form of arguments, prioritising porn over a partner or desensitisation to sex with a partner, it is nevertheless an issue that needs addressing. To address it, there needs to be a better understanding of what porn means to each partner.

Exercise

What does pornography mean to you?

* Do you watch pornography?
* Do you know why you watch pornography?
* Does your partner watch pornography?
* Do you know why your partner watches pornography?
* Does it impact on your sex life?
* If yes, is it in a positive or negative way? Please give examples
* Does it affect how you see yourself?
* Does it affect how you view your partner?

What have you learned about pornography in your relationship? Is it an issue? If so, you may choose to take some time out of your lives to sit down and talk about this issue and how it affects you both. What you have learned in the communication chapter and the empathy exercise will help you to talk about this with understanding, instead of being attacking or defensive from the start.

Once you have talked about this, try to find a compromise. If pornography is not that important to you, can you give it up for your partner? If not, would it help if it were no longer secretive? Do you both want to try to watch it together? These are just some of the ways that you could find a way forward.

If pornography is an issue for the person watching it and they cannot stop despite wanting to, professional help may be needed to look at the deeper underlying reasons as to why they cannot stop.

What would not be helpful or healthy for your relationship, is not looking at this issue and letting it forge an ever-increasing void between you.

Jealousy

Does jealousy cause issues in your relationship? Jealousy can be seen as the green-eyed monster or proof that someone cares. The word jealous comes from the Greek word 'Zelos' and means intensity of feeling.

But what exactly is jealousy? Let us have a look at it in more detail.

Jealousy is a perceived threat to something that you have an attachment to. Are jealousy and envy the same thing? The two are very different psychologically. You may feel envious that your colleague has been promoted over you, but you would not feel envious that your boyfriend is seeing an ex-girlfriend.

When you are envious, you want something that belongs to the other person. When you are jealous, you feel threatened by a third person that something is going to be taken away. Jealousy and envy can often be intertwined. For example, a man whose wife has cheated on him, may then focus on who she had an affair with. This is where envy may come in. The wife's husband may then wonder why she got involved with the other man and become envious of his job, looks, income. Anything that he feels is different or better than what he feels he offers.

Jealousy often originates during the Oedipal Stage (3-5 years of age) and envy can often originate from sibling rivalry. The way to understand jealousy better is to see where we lie on the jealousy scale. To be in the 'healthy' range, you need to be able to identify that there is indeed a threat to your relationship. Someone at the lower end of the scale may not see a threat, even if it is very obvious to everyone else. The upper end of the scale on the other hand, is the complete opposite. The person may see threats all around them where there are none. At the extreme upper end of the scale, you would have both acute and chronic jealousy.

Acute jealousy is when someone reacts to a threat in what would normally be an exaggerated and out of character way. These behaviours or ways of being tend to be displayed after a single event. Chronic jealousy, however, usually comes from childhood experiences or upbringing. A person who suffers from chronic jealousy tends to have low self-esteem and sees threats as being ever present.

If jealousy is present in the relationship, it is helpful for both of you to look at ways of changing negative habits and patterns and of dealing with it productively in your relationship.

Jealousy is a form of communication. What is it saying about you and your relationship?

Exercise

If there is jealousy in your relationship, the following questions will help you to have a better understanding of the role it plays between the two of you:

* Do you feel you are a jealous person?
* Using the scale we have spoken about above, where do you feel your jealousy lies? (Lower end of the scale, healthy, upper end, extreme, chronic…)
* Has your current partner ever cheated on you?

* Have you ever cheated on your current partner?
* Has a previous partner ever cheated on you?
* Have you ever cheated on a previous partner?
* If jealous, do you know your triggers? Please give examples
* Were you a jealous child or adolescent? Please give examples
* Do you compare yourself to others? (Status, looks, achievements…)
* If yes, how much do you compare yourself to others and in what way?
* Is jealousy negative, positive or both? Please give reasons for your answer

Having answered the questions above, do you feel that jealousy is an issue in your relationship? If your answer is yes, use the points below to work together with this issue so that you can both have a happier relationship without the devasting impact that jealousy can have.

The following ideas can help to reduce jealousy in your relationship. Each suggestion is applicable to both partners:

Communication

Be open with each other. Discuss what it feels like to be the jealous person and what it feels like to be their partner.

Understanding and empathy

No one likes the feeling of jealousy or of being accused unfairly

Reassurance

When the jealous person is feeling insecure, reassuring their partner that they are working towards being less jealous

Patience

Jealousy takes awareness, understanding and steps to address it

Important note:

If you find that jealousy is at the upper end of the scale such as chronic jealousy, seek professional help before doing any relationship work.

Chapter 5

Sex and intimacy

'Intimate relationships need to be built on a foundation of honesty, trust, and attraction'

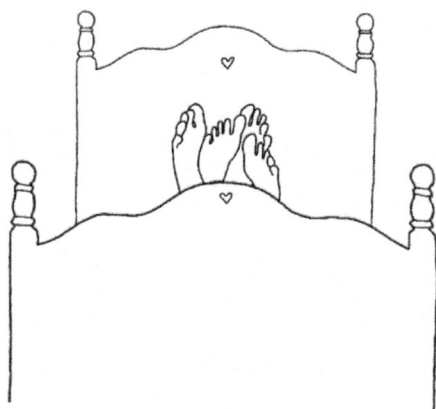

Sex and intimacy are an issue with many of the couples who come to see me.

If you would like to reconnect with your partner on a sexual and intimate level, this chapter is for you.

A helpful place to start is whether you both have similar thoughts, likes and dislikes when it comes to intimacy and sex.

Answering the following questions together will help in starting a discussion on this subject. Even if you are doing this exercise alone, you will have a clearer idea where your differences may lie. Please note that the answers to the following questions may change through the course of your relationship. Factors such as children, health, stress and medication can all drastically impact your thoughts and feelings about intimacy and sex.

Exercise

A. How often would you choose to have sex? The same, more often, less than at present?

B. What does intimacy mean to you? A hug, holding hands, connecting on a deeper emotional level?

C. Does your sex life revolve around your needs, your partner's needs or are both your needs being considered?

D. What sexual positions do you like?

E. Do you have any fantasies? If so, do you feel comfortable sharing these with your partner?

F. Do you want to be more adventurous? If yes, give some examples

G. Do you want to be less adventurous?

H. What would you not feel comfortable doing?

I. Do you feel comfortable talking about sex? With a trusted friend, with your partner, in general?

J. Does sex have a negative association for you? If yes, please explain

K. Have you had negative/traumatic experiences with sex? If yes, do you feel it affects your sex life today?

L. Do you feel body conscious or body confident when having sex?

M. Do you masturbate? Is this in addition to a happy sex life or as a substitute for an unhappy one?

N. Do you feel your needs are satisfied?

O. Do you view sex as a chore?

P. Do you both have the same libido? If not, did you use to be the same? What changed?

Q. Who usually instigates sex? Are you happy with this?

R. How important is sex to you?

S. How important is intimacy to you?

T. Are your partner's actions and words towards you positive with regards to sex and intimacy?

U. Are your partner's actions and words towards you negative with regards to sex and intimacy?

V. Do you need to feel emotionally close to have sex?

W. Would you have sex even if you did not want to?

X. Is sex used as a tool in your relationship? To get what you want, to make you feel more secure or as a form of control? To keep the peace or to avoid bad moods?

What do your answers say about your love life?

Is this an area that you both need to talk about and work on?

It may be helpful to have a look at each of the above points in more detail now. This will give you a better understanding of how your love life became what it is today. What your personal likes and dislikes are and what you would like your couple sex and intimacy to look like in the future.

A.   How often we have sex varies greatly from couple to couple. One couple I worked with had sex once a year on a particular date and others had sex every day. As you can see from the examples given, there are no set ways of being. But the majority of couples that I see are somewhere in the middle.

There is no 'right or wrong' and comparing yourself with other couples is not a healthy pursuit. Many factors need to be taken into consideration such as libido, health, stresses, age and how happy a person is in a relationship. The answer to whether we would like more or less sex may lie in the state of the relationship. If you feel unloved or there is no trust, you may not want to have much sex. If you felt loved, desired and secure, you may feel very differently about your sex life.

B.   Intimacy can mean different things to you and your partner. For some, intimacy means a closeness. A meeting of the minds. You feel connected and at one with your partner. This may be through laughing at the same things, understanding your partner and feeling understood in return, having the same ideas, goals and dreams. This can then lead to sexual intimacy.

For others, intimacy starts with the sexual or physical connection and they find it easier to connect with their partner on a more emotional level once that connection has been made. Maybe the physical closeness makes them feel loved, needed and wanted. Does any of the above resonate with you or your partner?

C.   When you have two people's needs to consider, it can be a challenge to satisfy (literally!) both parties. The first and crucial step is knowing or discovering what **your own** needs are. If you are in tune with what you like, dislike and need, that is a positive and healthy foundation for a happy sex life. If you are unsure, it is time for you to go on a journey of discovery. It can be daunting to know where or how to start but discovering our likes, dislikes and needs are something we do on a daily basis. We get tired… so we rest. We tried that flavour of ice cream and didn't like it… so we know something more about ourselves. We feel sad and need comfort… so we have a cry or a hug.

Discovering our intimate and sexual needs is a similar process. The difference is that a lot of the time, we make those everyday discoveries by happenstance and not with intent. We need to take some time out and discover what makes us happy and fulfilled sexually.

D.   When it comes to sex, preferences such as sexual positions are very personal to the individual. For some, the answer may be 'the quickest and easiest one'. Another may find a particular position brings them to climax more easily. For others, there are no preferences – just whatever happens in the moment.
The answer to your sexual preferences may bring about more awareness. For instance, should your preference be 'the quickest and easiest position', what do you feel that says about your sex life? Are you having as much enjoyment from it as you could be?
There may be other factors such as finding a position painful for example. You may wish to seek a doctor's advice if you are experiencing pain during sex.
If you have developed a trust and connection between each other, discovering what you like and dislike together may enrich and reawaken your sex life.

E.   Fantasies are not always easily talked about in relationships. Fear, ridicule or embarrassment are some of the reasons behind this.
Do you have fantasies that you would like to share with your partner but you don't know how to broach the subject? Trust features a lot when we talk about any subject related to sex in a relationship. For you to be able to share and talk about some of the things you would like to do or happen in your sex life, you need to feel confident that you will not be shamed or ridiculed. Knowing that your fantasies will remain private between the two of you should you wish this to be so, is also important.
So, when looking at fantasies, we really need to look at trust first. If you feel you are in a safe, loving and supportive relationship, you may want to gently start exploring these fantasies by talking to your partner about them.
As always, time and place are key. Your partner concentrating on an

important work email may not be the best time to start sharing your sexual fantasy... I have heard similar situations in my therapy room and it results in the person talking about the fantasy withdrawing into themselves, and the other party bewildered at what was expected of them at that particular time...

F. Do you want to be more adventurous?
    What does that look like for you?
    Lack of confidence can be an issue when it comes to being more adventurous. As with fantasies, you may fear being shamed or ridiculed if you suggest something out of the ordinary.
    Situations can also play a part, such as having children or caring for a parent in your home. Knowing you could be interrupted at any moment by a parent or child is not exactly conducive to wild, carefree sex. This is why the chapter on communication was at the start of this book. It is key to talk about what you both would like and how to realise those needs and wants that you both agree with.

G & H. It is important that you have a voice in your relationship. When it comes to your sex life, should something not feel comfortable or go against your way of being, you need to be able to voice this.
    This is a partnership. If you are being made to feel that you are 'not adventurous enough', you may want to look at your partner as well as yourself.
    Do you feel confident in yourself? Do you feel confident in your relationship?
    If not, does your partner help to make you feel more confident or less so?

I. Do you feel comfortable talking to your partner about sex? Whether you are wanting to address an issue or look at being more adventurous, **when** you talk about sex can play a big part in the responses you might get. It is usually best to talk about sexual issues at a neutral time and in a neutral location. Bringing up any concerns just prior or after sex may not be listened to in the same way as if you discuss it together away from the bedroom.
    How it is discussed is also key. Go back to the chapter on

Communication to refresh your mind on the best way to broach a sensitive subject. Starting with 'I feel..' statements are usually received better than 'You always/never...' statements.

J. Sex can be associated with positive and negative feelings. These may be derived from childhood, past relationships or what you have seen in the media. If sex has negative associations, it may be worth looking at what is behind those thoughts and feelings.
    You may find that you see sex as a negative as it causes you anxiety. You may, therefore, shy away from sex in order to avoid those anxious feelings. If you had an unexpected pregnancy, this may affect how you view sex. These are just a couple of examples of how our view of sex can be affected, but with love, trust and understanding in your present relationship, those associations can change to positive ones. The key here is to understand that the feelings you felt about sex a while ago, do not need to apply today.

K. If you have suffered a traumatic experience related to sex, it can have a profound impact on your relationship and sex life. In many ways, trauma and its aftereffects are not always seen to the naked eye. In the same way that physical abuse would be more easily seen and, therefore, potentially have more understanding and empathy, emotional abuse is not so visible and so there may be a lack of empathy or understanding as a result. The bruises and scars are internal, but they are still there.
    Some of the ways trauma can affect a person is that they may dissociate (become numb and detached from that situation) in order to be able to 'get through' sex. At the other end of the scale, they may want rougher, more intense sex in order to feel something. They may experience flashbacks of their trauma during sex.
    If you or your partner have experienced any form of sexual trauma, you may wish to seek professional help in order to be able to heal and have the relationship, sex life and peace that you deserve.

L. Lights on or lights off. One sexual position rather than another. With underwear or naked. Are these decisions made with sexual enjoyment in mind or as a result of low body confidence?

If you are busy thinking 'I need to lie down as I look better that way' or 'my….is/are not big enough…too big…not firm enough…not muscly enough…', you are not focussing on enjoyment or your desires.

Body image affects many people. If you were lucky enough to have a childhood where the people around you were body confident and were positive when talking about other people's body image, you may have gained and retained a positive view of yourself. People who may not have been so fortunate and whose body image has been criticised, may have less confidence in themselves. You can also add to the mix, the images fed to us by the media, the images in some porn and the delights of being able to change an image digitally, so that what you perceive to be real is in fact a fictional image. I have worked with students and these issues are very real for the youth growing up in our world today. But whether you are 20, 50 or 100 years old, body image can be an issue. The answer may lie in discovering who **you** are and what **your own** personal style or way of being is. Do we really all want to be clones of one another? Have you ever met a person who was sexually attractive but maybe not in a 'conventionally' attractive way? Worth thinking about.

M. For some people, masturbation feels like their partner is cheating on them. It can feel hurtful that your partner is seeking gratification without you. For others, masturbation is seen differently. It is not seen as being the same connection that you have as a couple. It is seen as a connection with yourself.
Problems can arise in a relationship when both partners have a different viewpoint on masturbation. If there is an issue, this needs to be discussed together. Empathy is needed to try to understand each other's point of view. One issue can be the feeling that masturbation has replaced your sex life as a couple. This can lead to resentment and hurt. With a better understanding, a solution and compromise can be reached. Whether that is including it in your sex life as a couple or compromising in a way that feels right for you both.

N. I have covered needs to a certain extent in paragraph C.

The other point worth looking at is how do you know if your needs are being met?

Here are some indicators as to whether your needs are being met in your relationship:

* You find yourself seeking attention outside of the relationship
* You feel that you are becoming more and more resentful
* You have started to minimise your needs
* You are consciously not wanting to give attention, time or energy to your partner
* You feel neglected
* You have a low tolerance level when it comes to your partner and feel irritated by them
* You keep a 'needs not being met' mental score

If any of the above speak to you, it is time to take action and look at both of your needs in the relationship before some or all of the above points start to erode it.

O. Do you view sex as a chore? If you did not always feel that way, what changed for you? Most of us live in a very busy, stressful and demanding world. There is so much to think about, organise and put into action in our everyday lives. Worries, stress and the physical energy needed to run our lives can, at times, leave us running on empty. It is hard to want sex when the only energy we have left is reserved for crawling into bed and letting our head hit the pillow so that we can finally crash out and go to sleep. Or if you are in constant physical pain, sex can feel like it is something 'else' you have to get through in your day, let alone enjoy. Time for self-care. There will be more on this subject in Chapter 6, but it is of paramount importance that you look after yourself in the best way that you can. Not for your 'partner, children, work, sex life…' but for **you.** Without you, what is this all for anyway? Treat yourself the way you would a loved one.

P.   Having a very different libido or sex drive can cause issues for some couples. Whether this was the case at the beginning of the relationship or has changed with time, it is important to find ways to talk about this in order to avoid any misunderstandings or feelings of rejection. I will look at libido or sexual desire in more detail further on in this chapter.

Q.   Does one partner usually instigate sex? If neither of you are instigating sex, it would be helpful for you both to look at the reasons for this. Is there a fear of being rejected? If this is an issue, the other partner needs to offer reassurance that when sex is initiated, their reaction would be positive and encouraging even if they decline sex on that occasion. As we have looked at in previous chapters, lack of sexual enjoyment may need to be looked at. Is the person who always instigates sex, controlling? Is sex always on their terms? Is this controlling behaviour apparent in other areas of the relationship? I look at controlling behaviours in a case study in Chapter 10.

R & S.   What does sex give you? Would you be missing something if you didn't have sex?
Can you have sex without intimacy? Can you be intimate without sex?
The answers to these questions may indicate how important sex is to you

T & U.   Do you make each other feel good when it comes to being desirable or your sex life in general? Do you compliment each other? Highlight the things you enjoy? Or do you make negative remarks about each other's body, or way of being sexually, and disguise these remarks as jokes?

V.   Some people are happy to have sex whatever the weather, whatever mood their partner is in and whether they look their best or worst. For these people, the connection is very much a physical one. For others, there needs to be certain things in place for them to feel sexually aroused. Feeling emotionally close is one of them. They would find it difficult to feel a connection if they were in a mood with their partner for example.

To have sex, do you need to feel emotionally close to your partner? Is your partner aware and sensitive to this?

W & X. Do you both feel good about your sex life or, does it, at times, feel more like you are 'servicing' your partner in order 'to have a peaceful life, to avoid bad moods, through feeling guilty of a wrongdoing'?

If sex is not connecting you together but is more of a bargaining chip or useful tool in your relationship, it is indicative of issues that need to be looked at. Either within yourselves as individuals or as a couple.

I am hoping the above points will help both of you look at your sex life in a new and positive way.

Looking at our sex life may not always be easy but it is worth it. For example, one of you may only feel like getting intimate when….not too tired….children are asleep….you like your body or when staying away from home. These are some of the common reasons given as to why sex is not high on the agenda. But it is often these very same clients who would like to have more intimacy and sex with their partners.

Realistically, if we were to wait until we were….less tired….or the children had flown the nest, liked our bodies or for our annual holiday, how long would you have to wait to reconnect on an intimate basis with your partner? How many times do we wait for the right moment? Meanwhile, life is passing us by. The key here is to change what can be changed and compromise on the rest.

Too tired, but you would like to rekindle your love life? Communicate this to your partner and then listen to their needs with regards to intimacy and sex. Could you give each other a break or help out more with chores or children?

Could you take time out to have a relaxing massage or take a long, relaxing bath? Or have a drink with a friend?

Important note:

These discussions are not a bartering tool whereupon one partner helps the other with the expectation of having sex in return.

Let us now have a look at some factors that can impact our sex life:

Libido

Libido or 'sexual desire' can vary and fluctuate greatly in a lifetime. Health, lifestyle changes, stress, medication, hormone levels, menopause and relationship issues are just some of the things that can affect our sexual drive. This can cause a 'desire imbalance' when one partner's sexual desire is higher than the other.

The first thing to highlight is the importance of not comparing our sex life to that of other people. What is 'normal' for one couple does not apply to another.

As long as both of you are happy with the frequency and quality of your sex life, that is where your focus needs to be. If you or your partner's libido is on a very different level and it is causing an issue in your relationship, there are strategies that can help with this. The first thing to establish is the root cause of the loss of sexual desire.

A low sexual desire in itself is not a problem. We all vary in our levels of sexual desires. It is only a problem if it used to be at a higher level and its decrease is causing distress in the relationship.

If you have a very different libido, it may cause an issue in your relationship, both of you would need to look at the loss of desire. If one of you no longer desires your partner or sex is not pleasurable for you, these thoughts and feelings would need to be looked at and acknowledged.

Communication

Revisit chapter 3 with this topic in mind. A lot of clients say that their partners do not know what they like or don't like. What is pleasurable or not pleasurable. Often, this is down to a lack of communication. It is also worth remembering that what may have turned you on at 22 years old may no longer be the case during your 50's. Talk to each other.

Hormonal changes

The menopause, monthly cycle, birth control and hormonal fluctuations can really affect a woman's sexual drive. A man's libido can be affected by low levels of testosterone and this can impact physical functionality. An imbalance in hormones can feel as though your body has been hijacked and can be very distressing for the person concerned. You may wish to seek medical advice if you feel your hormones are affecting your life in a negative way.

Physiological factors

There are many physical conditions that can impact your sex life. A visit to your GP may help in alleviating any concerns and treatment may be offered where necessary. A lot of medications can also lower the libido. For example, medications for diabetes, blood pressure and anti-depressants. If you are unsure, check with your pharmacist or GP as to whether your medication is playing a part in reduced sexual desire.

Health

Health plays an important role in our sexual desire. Lack of energy through not eating a balanced diet or from lack of sleep can be impacting. Men who are dependent on alcohol are more likely to experience long term sexual problems such as loss of desire, premature ejaculation and erectile dysfunction. Looking after your health can also increase your own confidence in how you feel or look.

Psychological

Whether you or your partner are feeling stressed, exhausted, depressed or anxious, your psychological state of mind will have an effect on your relationship. Including your sex life. It is worth looking at getting help with these issues for yourself, first and foremost but this will have a positive domino effect on your relationship and sex life too.

Circumstances

The mind and body may be willing, but the circumstances may not be helpful. Very young children, working away from home or a temporary injury are just some examples where you may want to have sex, but the situation you are in is affecting your sex life. The key here is to focus on the fact that you both have a desire to have sex and to keep that desire alive through communication. It is also through communication that you can look at your situation and see if you can plan around difficulties, such as some of the issues highlighted above. With no support system in place, could you pay for a babysitter? Have a day off in the week when the children are in nursery? Book to stay away with your partner if they are working away? Or be imaginative if your partner is 'out of action' through an injury for example.

The key is to find a way to create an intimate time with one another in what can be a busy, complicated and challenging life. Clients who have done this say that their relationship is all the stronger for it.

Here are some ways to reconnect with your partner in an intimate and sexual way:

* If you would like to rekindle your sex life but have a low sex drive, start with intimacy. Touch is a good starting point. Whether that is holding hands or laying across each other whilst watching tv, touch will physically and psychologically reconnect you.
* What do you like? Have you ever really spent some time thinking about what you like? Voice these likes to each other.
* Do you find that you both have a 'go to' position? What would it be like to instigate something different?
* For a lot of people, the difficulty lies in 'switching off' from the world. It is difficult to get lost in the moment if you are thinking that you need to buy some potatoes for dinner. Focus on your enjoyment.

* People change. Bodies change. Clients have often said that they can feel body conscious in certain positions. Talk to each other. If you feel your partner is feeling self-conscious, reassure them in a positive and genuine way.
* If belittling or shaming is present, so will a lack of abandon and confidence.
* Trust. Whether that is trusting each other in the relationship as a whole or trust whilst having sex.
* Do you have any fantasies that you would like to share with your partner? You may be pleasantly surprised by their reaction.
* You may wish to look for products that can help your sex life. Age, medication and a low sex drive can affect how your body responds to sex. There are many products and aids that can help you to have the sex life that you both desire.

Together, we are looking to implement changes in your relationship that improve wellbeing as well as your life as a couple. This includes a reconnection between the two of you.

Too much, too little, too adventurous, not adventurous enough. Whatever you would like to change, it will be up to both of you as a couple to identify where the differences lie, based on the exercises in this chapter. And to find new ways of approaching these differences. If you found yourself belittling your partner because you are feeling resentful, try to focus on their positives as a starting point.

These changes need to be discussed beforehand. It is a lot easier to instil changes in a relationship if you are both onboard. If your partner is not in the right headspace to look at making changes, you can always see what the dynamics are like when you respond in a non-defensive, positive and proactive way. This is sometimes enough to change their responses and behaviours towards you.

Think of your sex life as it is today. Now think of it being the best it can be.

Chapter 6

What about me?

'Looking after ourselves is not selfish.
It is self-care'

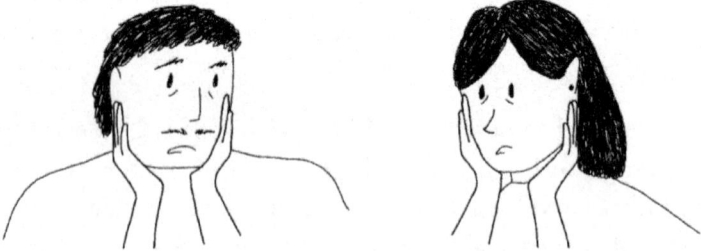

It may seem out of place to include a chapter about your own individual health and happiness in a relationship book but there are two people in a relationship and it is key for both to be happy within themselves.

You cannot have a happy and healthy partnership if one of you is unhappy or unfulfilled.

So, in this chapter, we will focus on your needs as an individual.

A lot of my clients have stated that they have lost themselves and do not really know who they are anymore. Work commitments, rent or mortgage payments, having children, blending families, parents, health can all impact in challenging ways.

See if any of the statements below resonate with you...

* 'I don't have any 'me' time anymore'
* 'I don't find anything exciting'
* 'I tend to follow my partner's lead in what we do'
* 'I feel I give a lot but don't receive much in return'
* 'I have stopped doing the hobbies and sports I used to enjoy'
* 'I don't socialise much or at all'
* 'I don't look after myself in the way I would like to'

Each statement that speaks to you is highlighting an area that needs attention.

Exercise

This coming week, choose one of the points above or one of your own and put something in place that would turn that particular point around. If you cannot action it this week, please book or diarise a particular date when you will take action.

Maybe you have stopped going to the gym because finances are tight. Could you go walking or running instead? Making time to play golf, read a book, have a manicure, can have a positive domino effect on your life. You feel more in control of your time and your life, are happier and therefore this translates into your life as a couple too.

These may sound like obvious solutions, but it is often the obvious solutions that are rarely implemented and yet have the biggest impact on our lives. This is not to say that one round of golf or a manicure will resolve all issues and create total happiness (wouldn't that be great?), but it is a start. Each positive action that you choose for yourself adds up.

How much time you spend on yourself has a direct impact on the relationship. A couple is made up of two individuals. Two unhappy individuals do not equate to a happy couple. Individual needs will differ from person to person. One person may need a couple of hours a week, another more like a day. Whatever your needs are, it is important to be able to voice them to each other.

Exercise

Do you know what your needs are? Doing the following exercise may help you to clarify these needs:

* Do you find that socialising recharges or depletes your energy levels?
* Do you enjoy your own company?
* Is there something you would like to do if you had more time or money?
* Do you feel lonely when your partner is not around?
* Do you both have similar needs when it comes to time alone?
* Do you have equal amounts of free time?

Time alone can be an opportunity to sit back and reflect on your thoughts and feelings. When you have catered to your needs, you may feel less resentful responding to your partner's needs, especially if free time is scarce for both of you.

What is the relationship with yourself like? How well do you know yourself? Do you know the parts of you that you try to conceal from others? Do you know the reasons behind this? These questions will need some self-reflection.

It is very common for people to look to others to heal their pain, to make them laugh or to support them in their hour of need. That is giving away an awful lot of power to others. Of course, this is part of relationships. To support and care for the other. But it is when that support or validation from your partner is expected, or you cannot function without it, that it needs attention. When you take ownership of yourself, you will also be taking ownership of your part in the relationship. The good, the bad and the not so nice parts.

How to begin to regain our own power is through awareness. Awareness of self. What do you like, respect and cherish about yourself? What do you not like about yourself? The process of self-awareness followed by self-acceptance is exactly that – a process. The views and thoughts you have about yourself will not change overnight, but by challenging those limiting beliefs, you will be able to appreciate yourself as a whole.

Neural pathways

It is worth noting at this point that we have neural pathways in our brain. I will use the path analogy as it may explain these pathways more clearly.

Neural pathways in your brain are a bit like paths you walk on.

A person may find themselves always choosing the same path to get back home. Even if they have several other paths to choose from, they tend to go for the one that **'is familiar', 'I was told this one was the best one for me', 'it is the path that my friends use', 'I'm too scared to use another path'**. Eventually the path would have a deeper groove and be more established as a path. The person would no longer think about the other paths and just automatically go down their chosen path.

Now, let us change the path to a neural pathway in our brain.

In the same way that the person finds themselves always choosing the same path, they can find themselves choosing the same thoughts. Even though they have the choice of many other thoughts, they will keep having that same thought because it **'is familiar', 'I was told this thought was applicable to me', 'it is the thinking that my friends use', 'I'm too scared to think differently'**. Eventually the neural pathway would be more established. The more that person thought a particular way, the stronger the neural pathway. The person would no longer think about other ways of thinking and just automatically have the same thought.

Neural pathways explained

* You think you do everything wrong = A new negative neural pathway is created
* You keep thinking you do everything wrong = That new negative neural pathway gets stronger
* You challenge those negative thoughts by thinking of the things you do well = A new positive neural pathway is created
* You think more positively about yourself = The new positive neural pathway gets stronger and the negative one gets weaker as a result.

How wonderful to know that we **can** change our negative thinking about ourselves and that we **can** create new positive pathways as a result!

Anxiety

You may wonder why a section on anxiety has been included in the self-care chapter. Since becoming a therapist, over a four year period, I have noticed clients reporting a sharp increase in levels of anxiety.

The following are very much my own thoughts and findings during this period and not based on an official study. Life has changed a lot since the 70s and 80s (if you are old enough to remember them as I am) When we wanted to contact someone, we needed to **wait** until office hours to be able to reach them. Now, a lot of my clients answer emails from their bed at gone midnight.

If you wanted to have a document signed, you would post it and **wait** for it to be returned. Even faxes were **slow**!

You had **limited choice** (four) when it came to tv channels. Now, we have the choice of over 400 channels.

If you wanted to watch a series, you would have to **wait** a week to watch the sequel.

Modern technology has a great deal of positives going for it. Many lives have been saved because of it. Contact between families who live apart, as well as setting up and running your own business, has never been easier. But I am looking at anxiety… and on this topic, the pace of life most of us live on a day-to-day basis creates heightened anxiety.

See if the following examples speak to you:

* I carry my mobile phone with me wherever I go
* I feel anxious if my phone isn't with me at all times
* I feel I need to answer texts and emails straight away
* It is expected of me to answer texts and emails straight away
* I watch TV and my phone simultaneously
* When I have a question in my mind, I need to know the answer as soon as possible
* My brain is switched on from the moment I am awake to the moment I go to sleep
* I watch social media and compare myself positively to others
* I watch social media and compare myself negatively to others
* Whether I am on a train, in a car, eating out or waiting for anything, I will be on my phone
* Whether I am on a train, in a car, eating out or waiting for anything, I will be taking in my surroundings and be present in the moment.
* I will spend hours on any form of technological device
* I will spend hours doing something I love

If you feel very anxious, one of the issues could be that your brain is being overstimulated. I am not looking at you living in the dark ages for the rest of your life, but you may want to make some very powerful and impacting changes to your life.

The following are some ideas that may help your anxiety:

* Create some new boundaries for yourself and for others.
* Limit the phone use when watching TV together at night-time .
* Have your phone on silent or vibrate unless you are waiting for a call
* Limit your social media time to a set amount
* Edit what and who you follow. Do you feel energised, uplifted and happy after seeing it? Or anxious, depressed and demotivated?
* Learn to be more present in the moment. This is especially true if travelling.
* Connect more with people, animals and nature
* Learn to switch off your brain. When your brain is 'on' from morning until night, it is like demanding your body to run a marathon **all day.** Your brain needs to rest to be able to work efficiently.
* Meditation, mindfulness, walking, being absorbed in an enjoyable pastime – these are all good antidotes for anxiety.

If you suffer from anxiety, it would be difficult to put most of the other self-care ideas we have looked at in place, as anxiety tends to overshadow how you think, behave and what you do or don't do. It is worth working on and starting to free yourself from that shadow.

Now, time to look at you… Do you have a good understanding of what you like about yourself or are not so fond of? Again, awareness and a deeper understanding of self is key to being happy 'in your own skin'.

Exercise

Using the example below, list 10 things that you like about yourself and 10 things you do not:

I like that I am… (For example: caring, tall, petite, good at maths, good at problem solving, thoughtful, a good listener…)

1.

2.

3.

4.

5.

6.

7.

8.

9.

10.

I do not like that I… (For example: am an unhealthy weight, feel not good enough, am always late, have not achieved my goals, am irritable a lot of the time…)

1.

2.

3.

4.

5.

6.

7.

8.

9.

10.

Now look at your statements as if you were in a court of law.

I would now like you to give evidence to confirm whether your statements are accurate or not. So, for example, 'I like that I am a caring person. The evidence would be that I am a nurse and care for people on a daily basis and I get positive feedback from patients that I am a caring person'.

If you like being petite, what are the enjoyable aspects of this?

Using the example 'that I do not feel good enough', do you have evidence that you are indeed good enough? Have you ever had positive feedback from someone, passed a test or exam, passed an interview, felt warmth or love from another person?

If you do not like the fact that you are always late and have the evidence to confirm that this is a problem in your life, such as having been reprimanded at work because of it, this is an area in your life that needs attention.

Having done the exercise, which thoughts about yourself were you able to challenge and which points need attention? Challenge the negative perceptions about yourself. If you still find they are an issue, work on these areas to become the best version of you.

To reach a level of acceptance of self is one of the greatest gifts that we can give ourselves. To fight things we cannot change, such as past events, certain aspects of the way we look or certain situations is waste of energy. Energy that could be used to change the situations, you want to change, to enjoy what your body and mind can do and to heal from past events if necessary.

Who are your role models? Do you admire strong, courageous and positive people or people who rely solely on their youth, physical attributes or monetary worth for their happiness and validation? These are fragile currencies. Looks and age will change and if it is your only currency, you may live in fear of your currency decreasing over time. Financial situations can also change during a lifetime. Then what? What will be left? It is important to embrace ourselves as a whole. Not just one facet of ourselves and not solely to rely on outside factors either.

We live in a world where discrimination and judgement still exist and unless you have experienced it yourself, it can be hard to truly understand just how impacting this can be. This is another reason why acceptance of self is so important. When others, including partners, put you down, belittle or ridicule you, it highlights their lack of self-worth. If they were truly at peace and confident in themselves, there would be no need to put anyone else down.

Exercise

In the following exercise, I would like you to think of a role model. Think about everything that has been discussed in this chapter.

* What qualities would that person need to have to become your role model?
* Do they have similar qualities to you?
* Are they similar to you in any other way?
* What do you admire about them?
* What makes them the way they are?
* Have they overcome obstacles in their life?
* How did they overcome these?

* What would it be like for you to be someone's role model?

Whilst the process of self-acceptance is taking its course, I am a firm believer in 'fake it until you become it'. Your mind will tune in very quickly to the way you behave, the actions you take and the words that come out of your mouth.

Imagine what messages you are sending to your brain with the following example:

Body language – Shoulders hunched, eyes cast to the floor

Voice – Quiet and only speaks when asked a question

Message to the mind – I am not confident. I have nothing important to say

As opposed to:

Body language – Shoulders back, standing straight, looking at people in the eyes

Voice – Clear and in a positive tone of voice

Message to the mind – I am confident. What I have to say matters

What messages do you send to your brain on a daily basis?

Do these messages challenge the negative thoughts you have about yourself or do they confirm them in your mind?

Fast forward to your golden years. What imprint would you like to have made on others and the earth? Would you like to look back and be proud of who you are and have been? Bring that forward to today. What would you need to put in place to become that person? If you have reached your golden years and are reading this, know that it is never too late to make changes in your life. Even the smallest of changes can make a big difference.

List below the 'ingredients' to your ideal future self and the life you would lead:

* What would your home life be like?
* What sort of relationship would you like with your partner?
* If applicable, what sort of relationship would you like with your children?
* What sort of relationship would you like with your family?
* What sort of relationship would you like with your friends?
* Would you like to retire or would you prefer to continue working?
* If applicable, what would retirement look like?
* What hobbies or interests would you like to enjoy?
* Would spirituality be a part of your life?
* How would you like to look after yourself physically?
* How would you like to look after yourself mentally?

What words would you want to be used to describe you in an epitaph? Do you want to be remembered as a good parent, a leader in your field, as caring and kind?

I often ask this question to clients. It is hard to know what road to take in life when you do not know the destination. This question can help you to know what you would like that destination to be like.

Chapter 7

Reconnecting

'Connection is the bridge of support, love and understanding that links you and your partner'

Everything we have looked at so far has been focused on awareness, understanding and problem solving.

Here, we are going to look at reconnecting you as a couple. What does reconnection mean to you?

Does it mean being able to go through a day or a week without arguing? Does it mean understanding each other so that both of you react to situations with more empathy? Or is it more love and sex in your relationship?

All of the above?

Exercise

Think about how you will be able to measure and know that your partnership is back on track and write it down.

For example, you may want your relationship goals to look like this:

A. Before my birthday, I would like us to communicate better on a day-to-day basis.
B. In a month's time, I would like to be sitting together on the sofa every Friday night without our phones on to distract us.
C. In six months' time, I would like to feel the trust is starting to be rebuilt.
D. In a year's time, I would like to be happy together, not feel the need to discuss the affair and for it to no longer trigger me.

The above are just examples, not set time frames, for you to adhere to. This exercise will help you focus on what you would like from your relationship. In the same way that clients come to see me for a check-in session, using time frames can help you to see how you are progressing in your relationship. If you are not where you were hoping to be by a particular time frame, see this as information. It is what you do with this information that counts.

When clients come for their check-in sessions, we will review how their relationship is progressing. If they are starting to slip back into old habits, we will use this knowledge or information and explore the reasons behind this.

Exercise

This is something you can both do using the points below:

* Set some relationship goals together
* Set some realistic time frames for each goal

Then write these down in your diaries or calendars.

If the goals were not met in the time frame, ask yourselves the following questions:

* Were the goals achievable?
* Were the time frames realistic?
* What were the main issues or obstacles in reaching your goals?
* What are healthy and positive ways to solve or overcome these?

During the first session, I explore how the couple first met. This can be very informative and can have an imprint on their relationship as a whole.

Here are some examples:

Meeting: By having an affair with their partner

Possible impact on relationship: The knowledge that their partner has the capability of having an affair and therefore trust may be an issue.

Meeting: Childhood sweethearts

Possible impact on relationship: Individuals grow and change all the time. But there can be some significant changes after your teens, going into adulthood. This can be challenging if the relationship was formed before these changes take shape.

Meeting: On the party scene

Possible impact on relationship: If alcohol and drugs were a large part of your relationship at the start, it may have influenced the way you see each other. You may have seen each other as carefree and fun loving. When the alcohol and drugs are not present, partners may then discover other facets to their partner. How they are in everyday life may be very different to how they met.

Meeting: Coming out of an abusive relationship or having experienced a traumatic event

Possible impact on relationship: If you have experienced an abusive relationship or trauma, you may feel that your partner 'rescued' you from that situation or made you feel safe. Once you have healed from the trauma, you may find that you do not have much in common with your 'rescuer'.

How did you both meet? Were there any challenges regarding the way you met or due to any other factors at the time? Are these things affecting you today?

When most couples meet, there is usually a honeymoon phase. Which of the following behaviours or thoughts applied to you or your partner:

* You were interested in what they had to say
* You made an effort with your appearance before seeing them
* You flirted with your partner
* You listened to your partner when they were talking
* You were tolerant of annoying behaviours
* You were looking forward to seeing them again
* You found them… attractive, funny, charming, sexy, kind….
* They were a priority in your life

Looking at the examples above, reflect on your relationship when you first met, what it is like today and how you would like it to be in the future.

We all evolve and change through the years. Circumstances also change and these can really affect a person's behaviour, way of being, tastes and goals. The key is to keep the connection alive between the two of you. Find and focus on the things that you do connect with. Your history together, shared memories, things that you both connect with today. If you are struggling to find any connection today, it may be that some new connections need to be discovered and created for the both of you to enjoy.

A big part of reconnecting with each other means making your relationship a priority and spending time with one another.

How much time do you devote to each other? Is it a priority in your life?

Exercise

In the following exercise, please include time spent and the kind of activity during the last week, where appropriate.

* Write down how much fun and relaxation you have had as a couple
* Who plans any time you spend together?
* By choice, how much time would you like to spend with your partner?
* What did you do for fun and enjoyment when you first met?
* Are you aware of the joys, the successes, the stresses, the disappointments and sadness in your partner's life at the moment?
* Do you enjoy each other's company?

Connecting with each other does not necessarily mean getting all dressed up and having the official date night – though that is good too – it can mean connecting with a hug, over a cup of tea or glass of wine without the distraction of TV or phones.

I appreciate that few of us have the luxury of time, so whilst I'm on the subject of reconnecting with your partner, here are some ideas that I give to my clients, but have fun and be imaginative with this.

Important note – if your relationship has broken down, is acrimonious or just not ready for doing things together, start as an individual and look at ways that you can include fun and relaxation in your life.

The issue

* Don't communicate well or at all. Quickly turns into arguing

Suggestion

*   Whilst you are working at your relationship, you may wish to go out of your home environment, to the cinema for example. You are together but without the potential for discussions turning into arguments.

The issue

*   Both exhausted and tired

Suggestion

*   You may find going to a restaurant helpful – no cooking or washing up!

The issue

*   No babysitters or support in place

Suggestion

*   Have a takeaway with a difference – whether that is trying out a different style of cuisine, setting up a small table in another room of the house or dressing up for that evening

The issue

*   Different work shifts

Suggestion

*   A loving gesture or action such as a note on the dashboard of the car. A favourite meal. Doing a job around the house unexpectedly. Something that tells each other that you are in each other's thoughts. (If you are at the receiving end of these gestures, be grateful for them. They may not be right or enough in your eyes, but they are a start and if they are not appreciated, they will stop altogether.)

The issue

* No intimacy

Suggestion

* Communication may need to be worked on first before you are able to look at the intimacy in your relationship but whilst you are working on it, you may try to reconnect by sitting together on the sofa or holding hands. Intimacy is different for every couple, so you need to find a comfortable starting point for both of you.

There are many other ways that you can start connecting and the above are just a few suggestions. You may feel that some are obvious, but what I have found in the sessions, is that couples know all of the above, but because life is so busy, it takes a professional to highlight or suggest things for them to be actioned and implemented.

One of the things that I do when I work with couples is to set homework, and at times the reaction is 'It feels so staged and false'. But think of it this way, if a doctor said you needed to exercise to save your life, chances are that you would put a plan in place and the benefits would outweigh the inconveniences. It is the same with relationships. Relationships are like plants – feed and nourish them or they will die.

So what **homework** could you set your relationship?

Start with something small that you both agree with.

Reconnecting with your partner, means knowing each other's needs.

Exercise

Look at the exercise below and tick where appropriate

Partner 1 – My needs:

* Companionship
* To be hugged and receive affection

114

* To be respected
* To be understood
* Friendship
* To feel loved
* To be sexually content
* To have help around the house
* To receive compliments
* To be given space
* To be an equal
* To be kissed
* To feel supported
* Trust
* Same values
* Same morals
* Quality time together
* Words of affirmation
* Cleanliness (house, self)
* Loyalty
* To have a motivated partner
* To have an ambitious partner
* Other…

Partner 2 – My needs:

* Companionship
* To be hugged and receive affection
* To be respected
* To be understood
* Friendship
* To feel loved
* To be sexually content
* To have help around the house
* To receive compliments
* To be given space
* To be an equal

* To be kissed
* To feel supported
* Trust
* Same values
* Same morals
* Quality time together
* Words of affirmation
* Cleanliness (house, self)
* Loyalty
* To have a motivated partner
* To have an ambitious partner
* Other…

Now, together, look at the exercise you have just completed. Were either of you surprised by some of the statements that were ticked or not ticked?

Discuss these together with the title of this chapter in mind 'Reconnecting'. What can you both do or say from having seen each other's answers that can help you both to reconnect and become closer as a result?

Your lifestyle

The way we run our lives can be very impacting on our relationship, both positively and negatively. Lack of sleep, feeling things are out of control, whether that is with housework or finances, may contribute to problems in your relationship. It may seem irrelevant to talk about health or work, but the ingredients in our life affect us as individuals and this can have a domino effect affecting our relationship with our partner, children, as well as ourselves. If you are unhappy at work or are not meeting your own needs, this will impact how you see life, how you behave and how you react to events around you.

Most of us will be able to understand and see why affairs or finances can impact a relationship, but housework is right up there with them. It was interesting to me when I first worked with couples, to discover just how impacting the subject of housework and the division of labour was within relationships. This is usually borne out of busy lives where time is precious and resentment builds if one party feels they are doing more than the other.

I would like you to think of your daily life now and discover which areas may need some attention.

Daily routine

*   Do you have a daily routine? If so, is it something you have made conscious decisions on or did it just come together by happenstance?
*   If you do not have one, would it be helpful to have one in place, or do you feel not having one is more beneficial for you and your partner?
*   Do your days include some me-time?
*   Do they include couple time?
*   Are you looking after your health on a daily basis? If yes, what does that look like? If no, what would you like to put in place for your health?

Housework

*   Are you both happy with the division of labour?
*   Do you both have jobs not linked to the running of the house?
*   Who primarily looks after the children?
*   What is your cleanliness barometer? Does one of you like the house to be immaculate whilst the other is happy to have a more relaxed approach?
*   What were your influences growing up with regards to tidiness and cleanliness?

Health

*   Do either of you suffer from mental health issues?
*   If yes, in what way does it impact?
*   If applicable, is your partner understanding with regards to your mental health?
*   If applicable, does your mental health impact the relationship?
*   If applicable, does your partner's mental health impact the relationship?

* Are you proactive in looking after your mental health?
* Is your partner proactive in looking after their mental health?
* Are you more pessimistic or positive?
* Is your partner more pessimistic or positive?
* Do you or your partner feel physically unhealthy or out of shape?
* Does this affect you or your partner?
* Do you drink alcohol? If so, do you feel you drink more than you need to or is recommended?
* Does your partner drink alcohol? If so, do they drink more than they need to or is recommended?
* If yes, how does this impact your life and relationship?
* Do either of you take drugs?
* If yes, does this impact your life and relationship?

Again, look at your answers together. Which areas need more awareness, support, action? Which areas can you recognise as being strengths in your relationship?

If you have covered the exercises in each chapter so far, WELL DONE!

That is an amazing achievement. These exercises involve a lot of self-reflection, identifying where the issue lies and putting what is necessary in place.

Exercise

Now go back to chapter 2 and answer the questions to the exercises A & B again.

What areas still need attention? What are the positive changes that have been made so far?

These exercises have proven themselves to be EFFECTIVE and POWERFUL tools to help you get the relationship that you both deserve.

Chapter 8

Relationship Q&A's

*'The answer lies in asking
yourself the right question about
your relationship'*

In this chapter, I will look at some of the most common questions that come up in my practice room.

Q – How do you overcome gridlock in your relationship?

A – You would like a child, but your partner does not want children. You want to spend time together, but you like to go to bed early and your partner is a night owl. You want to socialise all weekend and your partner prefers to just stay in together. Some problems that you face within your relationship may not be 'fixed' in an instant. Some compromises are difficult to make and when you are in gridlock it means that you have attached a lot of importance to whatever is at the heart of the issue. For example, going to bed early may mean that you will be able to get up early and get things done. If you are feeling that life is overwhelming and hugely stressful, this change can enable you to gain control back in your life.

It is important to talk to each other about what lies behind the issue. Why the subject at hand is important for you and what it means to you as a person. If you know something is important to your partner, ask them why it is so important to them. Try to empathise and not approach the topic by feeling that 'you have heard it all before'.

Once you have opened up to each other and have a better understanding of the reasons why this is so important, see if a compromise can be reached. Gridlocks can be so destructive to relationships. Being able to understand what is important to your partner and reflect this back to them may help to change and shift the gridlock. It is about taking into account their needs and wants as well as your own.

If you still find that after this process you are not able to compromise, such as whether to have a child or not, you need to think ahead in time. In twenty years' time, would the issue still be relevant? Would you have any regrets? How important is this relationship in relation to the issue at hand? These are tough questions to answer but a gridlock situation can last for years if not dealt with, as it will only fester and build resentment.

Q – Can couples still stay amicable after a breakup?

A – A few factors come into play when answering this question. It stands to reason that it would be much harder for a couple to stay friendly or even civil if one of the partners was cheated on. An amicable break up needs to be founded on some mutual respect for each other. This may be respect for what you once shared together or that your partner is the mother/father of your child.

If you want to break up but your partner does not feel the same way, it may mean handling the situation with sensitivity. Your partner may not know 'what they have done wrong', 'what can they do now that would change your mind', 'what was real and what was not throughout your relationship'. If you are both able to, it may be helpful to talk about where the relationship went wrong in order for both parties to have closure after the breakup. If you feel that you cannot or do not want to try to work on the things that broke up your relationship, it would be important to make this clear, so that your partner does not feel that there is hope and living their life in limbo whilst you have moved on.

Staying civil and respectful to each other is especially important in front of your children. Even if you cannot tolerate the sight of each other, if you have to interact in front of the children, you will be protecting them from a lot of hurt and uncertainty if you can be civil and respectful to each other.

Q – What happens if we now don't have the same future goals?

A – This can be a challenging one. You met. You both shaped this life together and talked and planned about the future. Suddenly, your partner has an accident which was a near death experience. They now want to blow your plans and live for the moment doing what they want to do.

You both plan for retirement and what you will do together. One of you is made redundant. Their job is very specialised, so it is difficult to go back into the workplace. The other partner now has to work full time and retire later than they had planned.

You were childhood sweethearts when you met. You both always dreamed of having a family and one of you was going to stay at home to look after them. Then, the chance of a lifetime comes up in your career. This involves a lot of travelling around the world, but you know it will fulfil you as a person. Suddenly, the idea of having children feels like a tie.

The real challenge is for you both to compromise in a way that you both feel happy and not feel as though you are tagging along to someone else's life.

We all change and grow throughout our lives. If your partner is more important to you than those changes, then it can work. Whether that is agreeing to one person's dream for a set time, then to spend some time on the other person's dream or trying to mesh the two as well as you possibly can.

After all, the dream job, the new house, the benefits of living in another country can all be valid, but you need to ask yourself if they are as valid if your partner was not sharing these experiences with you.

Q – What is controlling behaviour in a relationship?

A – Controlling behaviours come in many forms. It can be checking up on a partner in an unhealthy and repetitive way. 'Where have you been?', 'Why are you five minutes late?', 'What are you looking at on your phone?' All these in isolation are perfectly innocent questions to ask, but asked repetitively and with a sense of 'having a right to know' illustrates controlling behaviour.

Commenting on what you are wearing or what you are doing in order to manipulate you for example. 'So, who are you trying to impress at your works do?', 'You are not wearing that. It's only because I feel protective of you. I love you', 'Why did you buy yourself that dress? You know I like to buy you your clothes.'

Keeping a tight rein on the partner's independence is also a sign of controlling behaviour. Whether that means limiting access to money, friends or family. This enables the controlling partner to feel that they are relied on and, therefore, are more in control of their partner and their relationship as a whole. Shaming, embarrassment and belittling can also be used. This can often affect a person's self-worth which in turn makes it harder to get out of the situation that they are in.

When wanting to do something about a controlling partner, one of the first steps is to identify the behaviours. Start being aware of the things which are being said and challenge them **in your mind**. I emphasise 'in your mind' at first as some partners with controlling tendencies can be volatile and it is always best to keep your safety in mind first and foremost.

Once you have begun to identify the behaviours, start to see them for what they are 'lies and manipulations'. These behaviours are borne out of a lack of self-worth and therefore are not factual. They are an (unhealthy) tool that is used to make the controlling partner feel better about **themselves**. It has nothing to do with you.

If you are able to talk to your partner without feeling that your safety will be compromised, then it is worth 'naming the process'. This is when you highlight, in a factual way what they are doing. This is best done shortly after the event, rather than at the time:

Here are some examples:

Controlling behaviour – 'Why did you buy yourself that dress? You know I like to buy you your clothes.'

Possible response – 'It is nice that you buy me clothes, but I like to buy myself clothes too.'

Controlling behaviour - 'Why are you five minutes late?'

Possible response – 'Sorry? Late for what? I am just going about my day.'

In the same way that controlling behaviours are often the same and repeated, so can the 'I am standing my ground' responses.

The level of controlling behaviour will determine what is the best route for you to take. If you feel that your partner is overall a reasonable person whose insecurities translate into controlling behaviours, you may be able to talk about this issue together and work on reassuring them and they in turn, on reducing the controlling behaviours.

Important note: If, however, you feel fear and apprehension in your relationship, you may need to seek professional support whilst you choose to either work on this together or walk away from the relationship.

Q – What is considered cheating?

A – This will depend on the boundaries you have both put in place. Someone may see flirting with another as harmless fun whilst another person may find this offensive. I have worked with 'Open' relationships where both partners are happy to have other sexual partners. Yet issues can still come up either when boundaries have not been discussed and understood or when those boundaries are crossed. Do you and your partner know where your boundaries lie? For a lot of couples, it may seem obvious where the boundaries lie, but it is only after speaking and clarifying it with their partner, that they realise that a small misunderstanding on this subject, can have a big impact on the relationship.

To discover that your partner likes to stay friends with his ex-girlfriends may be something that goes beyond your own personal boundary of what is ok in a relationship. As with all the topics covered in this book, it comes down to better communication. The conversation you will have on this topic will be a lot easier to deal with than the aftermath of a broken boundary.

Q – Is arguing positive or negative in a relationship?

A – There may be times when it is necessary to confront and challenge your partner on a particular issue. It is how you discuss this issue that is important. If you argue in a healthy way, you can have your thoughts and concerns heard and come to an amicable resolution. It may not always 'go your way' but that will be the case with your partner too. This is compromise. Let us look at arguments in your relationship. Do you find that emotions are highly charged before you have even started talking? If so, it is important for you to pause and take stock.

If your emotions feel out of control, so will the argument. Couples who argue very frequently can lose the perspective on each argument. In other words, every argument receives the same emotional charge. Whether the cat litter tray has not been changed or the bailiffs have been knocking at the door. If your partner knows you will 'blow your top' at everything that needs to be resolved or discussed, they may well switch off to everything, making the situation even harder to look at and discuss for you both.

An important note is to argue in private. Arguing in front of children is very impacting. They look to their parents/carers to provide a safe and secure base. Negative arguing shakes those foundations. They often blame themselves for the arguments and are usually not present when the parents reconcile their differences, so they only tend to be exposed to the shouting, name calling and disruption in the household. In contrast, disagreements which are dealt with in a positive way can be very helpful for children to witness. It can be part of their learning on how to deal with their own disagreements or frustrations with other people as they grow up.

Another issue that fuels arguments is bringing up all the disagreements, unfairness from the past into a current discussion. Again, you will end up with a disproportionate argument which will result in disproportionate responses and a negative outcome. Arguments can then become personal too. What started out as a discussion on whether to see your in-laws this weekend or next weekend ends up with both of you hurling personal and character insults at each other.

Did the argument end with a resolution or is it unfinished business ready to be brought up again in the next argument? Try to look at the bigger picture. Is it that important to you or can you compromise?

Q – My partner is depressed and suicidal. What do I do?

A – This is a situation that faces many couples today. The pressures of life and financial expectations as you create a relationship, home and future, can and is overwhelming for many. There are two situations here. The first is if your partner recognises the way that they are feeling is having a negative impact on their life, as well as yours and children, if they have any. If they recognise that this is an issue that needs attention, then they would need to seek professional help. A therapist would be able to look at the issues troubling them and they would work together to alleviate, change or re-frame those issues. Suicidal ideations would also be looked at.

The second situation is if your partner is not able or willing to look at their depression and suicide ideation. This can be very challenging and distressing for both parties. A feeling of overwhelming helplessness for their partner and the inability to see a way out for the partner who is suffering from depression. In this situation, I would urge you to seek professional help yourself. This support will help you and your partner.

It is also important to note that, contrary to popular belief, people who talk about suicide are not any less likely to do it than people who do not talk about it. If someone says that they no longer want to be here, take them seriously and seek help and support for yourself and your partner.

Q – What do I do in an abusive relationship?

A – Abuse is violent or cruel behaviour towards another. This can be physical or mental. As I wrote in the introduction to this book, physical or emotional abuse has no place in a loving relationship. If you are in a relationship where there is a pattern of abuse, get professional help or get out of this situation now. If you have an emotionally abusive relationship, you need to seek help from a professional therapist who will help guide either you as an individual, or both of you if your partner recognises that they are in need of help.

Abuse can be so challenging for the victim. Are they going mad? Is it as bad as they imagine? Will they make it worse for themselves and their children if they leave? Whatever your situation, take action today. Make an appointment to see someone, call a support centre. Whatever steps you do decide to make, ensure that you are safe in doing so. Abusers have a tendency to 'get back to normal' in between episodes, promising that it will never happen again. The statistics and research on domestic violence show otherwise.

Q – Can a relationship ever recover from an affair?

A – The answer will very much vary depending on the couple involved. The short answer is yes if both parties are able and willing to look at their relationship as a whole and do the work needed to rebuild trust. It will also depend on whether the reasons for the affair have been explored and whether the person who has broken the trust is remorseful and is willing to do the repair work needed. There have been several instances where the person who had the affair is keen that 'I fix' their partner and help their partner to get over the affair as quickly as possible 'so that they can get back to normal'. I then have to highlight that it is not their partner that needs 'fixing' but the break of trust in their relationship and the responsibility for this lies with the person who has broken that trust and not their partner or the marriage counsellor. That is not to say that both of them do not have things that they need to look at to improve their relationship as a whole but, even if you feel you did not have enough attention in the relationship, it is not up to your partner to do all the work, as you had the affair 'because you felt unloved'. It is for the person who broke the trust to do the reparatory work to rebuild it and for the partner, in this case, to look at the part they played in their relationship and see if they also need to make some changes in order for both of them to move forward in a healthier way.

Q – How do I know if my relationship is over?

A – This will very much depend on how much work has gone into making the changes needed in your relationship. If you feel you have looked at your part in the relationship and your partner has also tried to make changes but you still feel a disconnect, it may be time to revise where your relationship is going. Whether you feel repulsion when they touch you or your partner says they want to remain faithful yet persistently breaks this promise. If they have an addiction and they are not willing to do anything about it. Whether it is gambling, drugs or alcohol, you are dealing with three elements in your relationship, not two. And unless they have persistently proved that they are trying to overcome their habit with a support agency or therapist, then it is time to move on.

There comes a time in a relationship when words are no longer applicable. Only actions will do. And when it comes to breaking trust, nothing will rebuild trust more than actions. Not all couples that come through my practice stay together. Sometimes, there has been too much hurt and repeated break of trust or not enough work done by one or both parties. Or they simply are too different as people.

Q – Can blended families work?

A – As the name implies, two people with children from a previous relationship coming together, are blending together. Except that, at times, the blending is more like oil and water. When this is the case, it is about focussing on having a basic respect for all the individuals involved. When a child is yours, you may overlook some misdemeanours or irritations in a way that may not be the case with a stepchild. What is worth remembering is that the children don't usually have a say in who their stepparents are. This can be very hard for them. Not only are they not with their own parents but they 'have to' adjust to this new person who has entered their lives.

Children can feel neglected or put out if a lot of attention is given to the parent's new partner. At times, the child has witnessed and experienced several blended families.

If you are getting together and blending a family as a result, it is worth noting that you may both have very different parenting styles. This needs to be looked at and discussed before moving in together. Overcompensating, being overly strict, favouritism or not caring for your partner's children's welfare are key points that you may need to look at together. This can be a very emotive subject and will need the communication tools you have learned in this book to be able to talk about these things openly and constructively. But most importantly, to talk about them with empathy.

As adults, when you decide to be with your partner, you decide to be civil and respectful to their children too. This may not always be reciprocated but hopefully, in time, they will also be civil or a closer bond may grow.

There can be real joy in having a blended family. If you do connect with your stepchildren, it is a privilege to be a support and friend to them. As they can be for you too.

Chapter 9

Case studies

'We can learn so much about ourselves through our relationships'

I will be using real examples and real people from my therapy room to demonstrate some of the challenges faced by couples and how these can be worked on. The whole case study may not be applicable to you but there may be elements that are, and these may help you to understand your relationship better.

Names, places and recognisable features and events have been changed to preserve anonymity.

Case study 1 – Communication

Steve and Vicky have been married for a few months. They came to see me as they were getting increasingly concerned that the communication between them had broken down. Steve felt he was 'losing Vicky' as, whenever they had a disagreement, she would withdraw and become distant. Sometimes, for days at a time. Steve felt he tried everything to get Vicky to talk. From Vicky's point of view, Steve had changed since they moved in together. They used to talk things through but now, she felt he just shouted. She felt as though she was always walking on eggshells.

After some exploration, we were able to see that Steve came from a family where shouting was commonplace. Whether they were having fun or arguing, the members of Steve's family would speak over each other and the louder they shouted, the louder they would respond in order to be heard. Vicky had never experienced this and for her the shouting felt very aggressive and threatening, hence her withdrawal. Her parents never seemed to argue and no one had ever raised their voice in her home growing up. She had always associated shouting with aggression or violence from what she saw on television. This was never highlighted as an issue when they were dating as they did not have anything to argue about. It was when they had both created a home environment of their own that things became noticeable.

Steve felt that he was unable to express himself. He did not feel that he was being aggressive or angry and this lead to a lot of misunderstandings between them.

Therapy was then based on recognising these differences and having a better understanding of each other and their needs. Understanding how shouting affected Vicky, Steve was able to work on talking to Vicky instead of shouting. Vicky worked on challenging Steve when he did shout, along with having a better understanding that shouting did not necessarily equal anger. Over time they both created a new way of talking and arguing that was healthier for them both and not based on their own life scripts.

Case study 2 – Resentment

Jo and Pippa have just moved to a new area with their two young children. They used to live close to their families and friends but wanted their children to live by the sea in a more relaxed environment. This meant a lot of changes for all of them. The move alone was stressful and very quickly impacted their relationship and family life. Jo had decided to start a new business which meant devoting 60-70 hours a week to get it off the ground. Pippa took care of their pre-school children, the running of the house and household finances. With no friends or family for support, they did not have a break and this caused resentment to build up.

The first session was initially filled with 'evidence' against the other with regards to their input in the running of their lives. At the same time, they would highlight what their own input was in comparison to the other. Although informative at first, as it gave me a window into their homelife, it was time to pause the session and reflect my observations back to them. Clearly, both worked really hard and both desperately needed a break. When time off is scarce, it becomes a precious commodity. Couples can end up arguing that one person had ten minutes more free time than the other. It can feel like survival. And when we are in survival mode, we tend to think of our needs first. But when in a relationship, both needs are to be considered.

At first, whatever we looked at or explored was met with a 'But'. 'But we cannot do that because we do not have time… But I have tried that already… But I do not think it is going to work…' It is important to look at 'what is' in a situation as looking at 'what it should be' can keep a couple stuck and unable to see a way forward. So, we looked at what would be needed for them as individuals, as a couple and as a family moving forward. Then we looked at the 'what is'. Finding a babysitter was not an option at that time so we looked at how they could support each other and work as a team instead of against each other.

They decided on giving each other two hours off each week where one would do something enjoyable away from the house (hard to switch off if a child is upstairs screaming) whilst the other looked after the children. They also made a point of having a 'movie/take away' night together each week once the children were in bed with no phones on to distract them.

From the first week of making some of these changes, they noticed a big difference. It can have a really positive domino effect. One small change can impact other areas. Having some time off for example, can recharge an individual which may then enable them to have more patience and energy to communicate with their partner in a healthy way.

Case study 3 – Things outside your control

Ian and Corine came to see me as Corine was suffering from the menopause and this deeply affected her and was starting to cause issues within their relationship. Ian was a builder and they had just moved into their 'forever' home, but it needed some renovation work. Corine's work was based at home and involved meetings online as well as a lot of telephone work. They had been together for ten years and married for eight.

They both loved each other very much and this was clear to see from the first session. The issue was the lack of understanding and awareness. Ian wanted Corine to recognise that her behaviour could, at times, be irrational or fuelled by the menopause and Corine was resentful that her menopause was now the reason for any disagreement or misunderstanding. The arguments had slowly built up over time and it came to the point that they were now constantly defensive towards one another. They would predict what the other was going to say. There was a lot of miscommunication on both sides. The words that were said were not received in the way that they were meant and resentment was slowly building up.

Corine had tried everything to improve her symptoms but her choices were limited to a holistic approach as there had been cancer in the family, so HRT was out of the question. Corine felt hijacked by her menopause and frustrated that Ian was unable to understand the impact it was having on her. Ian, on the other hand also felt he was being impacted by the menopause, but in a different way. He felt talking to his wife was like walking on eggshells. He could no longer see the Corine he knew whenever she reacted strongly to something and longed to have 'his' Corine back. I worked with both of them to increase the understanding of what it is like to be each other and they discovered that ultimately, both wanted the same goal. To be together and to communicate in a positive way.

There are events or situations in our lives that have a real impact, and we cannot always eradicate, solve, fix or change them. Both felt that they were trying their best but that the results still ended up with both of them arguing. Ian came to a better understanding that when Corine reacted in a certain way, she could not help it. The hormones, in this case, were dictating her moods or reactions. This was not, of course, all the time but they came to an agreement that Corine would approach Ian after an argument and they would then talk calmy about it and work together to see what was needed at that time. If Corine felt the argument was due to the menopause, Ian would then ask Corine if there was anything he could do to help – this then clarifies things for both as well as gets them working together rather than against each other. If the argument was based on anything other than the menopause, they would talk it through and listen to each other's point of view and try to resolve it together.

In this case study, it was the menopausal symptoms that created an issue for the couple. This is something out of both their control. You can base this study on other situations including a partner having a mental health condition such as bipolar and the impact this can have on an individual and the couple.

Case study 4 – Low self-worth

Pete and Susan had been together for twelve years before coming to see me. Susan had met someone online and had started talking to him for support. Pete found out and was devastated. He had never doubted Susan's trust in all these years. Through the sessions, we were able to see how Susan recognised that what she had done was not ok within their relationship, but what also transpired was that she had tried to communicate with Pete for several years now, that she felt taken for granted and not listened to. In the session, it was interesting for me to notice that whenever Susan highlighted this or another issue she had with the relationship, Pete interrupted her to say how he felt.

At this, she then became angry and said that this was the very core of the issue for her. It was all about Pete and always had been.

Susan was frustrated that even in a counselling setting, he was not hearing her. We explored this and Pete admitted that he did offload to Susan without ever asking how her day was. In the sessions, Susan was shown to be the family's rock and that she did everything for them. Through exploring their relationship, we were able to discover that Pete had never felt good enough for her and, therefore, had felt insecure about their relationship from the start. This meant that he had one foot in the relationship and one foot out. This way, he was 'protecting' himself from being hurt. He had been hurt and cheated on by his previous wife and girlfriends which then cemented his thoughts that he was not good enough as a person. Therapy work was undertaken on an individual basis with Pete to explore and help him to understand his lack of self-worth.

I also worked with them as a couple to improve communication between them. As the sessions went on, you could see Susan's confidence grow. She now had a voice in the relationship. Pete's confidence was also growing. Instead of feeling that all his happiness lay with Susan, he came to the awareness that he needed to find peace and happiness within himself first.

Case study 5 – Betrayal

Jenny and Mark have been married for over 20 years. Sitting in my practice room joking, laughing and being very tactile it would not be immediately obvious that this couple were on the brink of a break up and were in inner turmoil. Both were keen to highlight how good their marriage had always been and how they had always had a great sex life.

At first, when we started exploring how Jenny's affair came about, the questions were met with a blanket 'I don't know' answer. With further exploration, we were able to discover that Jenny had become increasingly invisible to Mark and when a colleague at work started talking and, more importantly, listening to Jenny, it made her feel alive again.

What started as a friendly chat quickly lead to a physical affair. Jenny told Mark soon after the affair started as she realised that she was not in love with her colleague, what she loved was the attention he gave her. The sessions that followed were similar to working with a bereaved client. Mark was in mourning. There are several losses when someone has an affair. Loss of trust, loss of thinking that your partner is not capable of having an affair, loss of time, as grieving takes time. The waves of different emotions that Mark described when he was told of the affair are also akin to a bereavement. Shock, numbness, anger, sadness, guilt can all be felt.

We spent the following weeks looking at how the affair started and Mark and Jenny were both able to express their thoughts to each other. Both decided to give their marriage a second chance and to put certain things in place to ensure that both their needs were being met. Jenny also needed to rebuild Mark's trust and we looked at ways to do this. Transparency was key to the rebuilding of trust. Mark needed to be able to ask Jenny to see her phone if he felt insecure. This is not something that Mark could do behind Jenny's back as this would then again affect the trust between them, but if feeling insecure, it would rebuild Mark's trust towards Jenny if he is able to see for himself that there was nothing untoward going on. I highlight to clients that at some point, you need to decide to trust that person. To live a life when there is a constant need to see your partner's phone is not healthy for either party long term.

They both worked on the relationship. It was not always easy for them. Triggers, questions and various emotions would, for a period of time, pause the progress. We would work through these together using the same method that you can use at home. Communication, understanding and empathy.

Case study 6 – Negative associations

Megan and Ben came to see me as they had found that over years together, they had no real disagreements apart from twice a year when they would have huge arguments and very hurtful things would be said along with shouting and screaming. These arguments left scars and they became harder to heal, eroding the relationship as a result. For the first session, the couple wanted to focus on the differences in their character as they felt that this was the main issue. It quickly transpired that Megan would 'hold on' to any wrongdoings throughout the year, only to unleash them during their bi-annual blow out.

In the sessions, Megan expressed feeling annoyed that she let so many things go throughout the year and when Ben criticised her for what she felt were trivial things, it caused a strong reaction of unfairness in her. Through exploration, we were able to discover that Ben had some negative associations to the care and attention Megan gave to the house they had bought together. On the surface, it looked like he was complaining that she was not doing her share of the housework but when we looked into the feeling associated with this, we were able to discover that it represented so much more.

Ben revealed that two years previously Megan had been unfaithful. When they moved in together, Megan would love to decorate and make their home feel welcoming. But after the birth of their baby boy, Megan had other priorities. Ben felt that her perceived lack of interest in their home was a direct link to how she felt about him. Lack of interest in the house equalled lack of interest in him and the relationship. He therefore feared that Megan would have another affair.

We looked at both Megan and Ben's thought processes and looked at communicating throughout the year to avoid the inevitable build-up of misunderstandings and resentments culminating into a very damaging argument.

This case study highlights how we can create negative associations with certain events, people or things and they can then act as emotional triggers. It is identifying what those negative associations and triggers are that is key. Once we have identified them, we can then talk, work on, heal or do what is needed to process these past hurts.

Case study 7– Busy lives

This is a very common issue with couples today. One couple came to see me after 16 years of marriage. They had 2 daughters and a son. They felt that the communication between them had broken down. Robyn felt a lot of anger towards her husband, Jack. She felt that Jack no longer respected her and took her for granted. Jack seemed very surprised at this and said he was 'unaware' that she felt this way. As far as he was concerned, they were not getting on as well as they could, but basically, everything was fine. This, for Robyn, was part of the issue. Jack not noticing. Not noticing the things that needed doing around the house. Not noticing the state of their marriage. Not noticing her.

We started to look at what each needed – as individuals and in the relationship. Doing this, revealed that both felt unappreciated. Jack was working long hours on his own business and Robyn also worked long hours for a demanding company. Then they had the children to look after, both had ailing parents as well as looking after the daily chores.

Here was the biggest stumbling block for the therapeutic work. They were both willing and keen to work at their relationship. But, what would happen is that each week homework would be set and both found it 'impossible' to find the time to put any of it into practice. The homework was reduced as a starting point but they still found it difficult to carve out even a few moments for each other. Something had to change.

In the session, I highlighted that having some time together was crucial to the success of their relationship. One hour a week in my practice room was not enough to work on the issues that they were struggling with. This was something that they were aware of all along, but they needed to hear it from a third party. They said it was as though 'I gave them permission' to put themselves first. The changes they made were not easy at first and took some negotiating but the immediate, positive effect it had on them as a couple quickly made the effort worthwhile.

Do you need to give yourselves permission in an area of your relationship?

Case study 8 – Loss of sexual desire

Chris and Julia have been together for 5 years. Chris wanted to separate. There was no intimacy left in the relationship. He felt they were living as flatmates. They used to have a 'great' sex life and now, they didn't have a sex life at all. Neither of them could pinpoint when it started to change.

Using the same questions that I have shared with you in the exercises set out in this book, we were able to discover that Julia had experienced a change of roles in the relationship. When they first met, Chris would always compliment Julia and they would frequently go out. All they would focus on was having a good time together. Then they moved in together and gradually, Julia found herself 'picking up after Chris' all the time. She felt more like 'his mother' now. From his point of view, Chris felt he was always the one to organise any outings or date nights.

So, Julia felt frustrated with Chris and Chris was frustrated with Julia. Instead of talking this through together, they made up their own versions of why they were being off with each other. 'they have gone off me', 'they can't be bothered with this relationship anymore', 'they disrespect me', 'they take me for granted'. And so, these thoughts became facts in their mind and mushroomed. Can you see how something that could be resolved fairly easily can then be mushroomed out of control through, at times, inaccurate thoughts and catastrophising?

These issues changed how they felt in the relationship. Once they understood this, they both worked on the issues at hand and on reconnecting in an intimate and sexual way.

Case study 9 – Blended families

James and Rita came to counselling as they were struggling with blending their family together. They had been together for four years and moved in together after two. Rita had two sons from a previous marriage. The issue for James was that he felt that his feelings were being side-lined. He felt that he was not being heard and so would withdraw from the relationship. Rita suffered from anxiety and was struggling with her own emotions as well as looking after her children. She felt she could 'not handle' James' feelings at the moment and that he was 'big enough' to deal with them himself. In the first sessions, I often ask each client what attracted them to each other in the first place. At times, the very things that you found attractive at the beginning of the relationship are the things that you are struggling with now.

Rita was attracted to James' ambition and drive. She liked his no-nonsense approach. But she then felt that with that drive and ambition came a lack of empathy, understanding and patience. Especially when it came to her children. She felt that he was taking but not giving.

James was attracted to Rita's kind, caring and gentle nature but felt that this translated into 'being overly sensitive and anxious' about her children and would not discipline them in the way he would. He also felt he was working hard to provide the extra money needed and felt unappreciated.

We worked on recognising what parts each of them played in all the positive elements of their relationship and then what parts they played in the issues that they had. Only when we had looked at and worked on the issues in the relationship, did we start to look at parenting styles and issues with regards to blending a family.

You may find chapter 2 helpful in looking at the parts you each play in your relationship.

Case study 10 – Living with a narcissist

Melanie's husband died five years ago. They had a long and happy marriage. She did not think that she would be in a relationship again. She wasn't looking for one having settled into her new life made up of friends, book and gardening clubs and a part-time job. Then Bill came into her life. He used to come into the cafe where she worked. He was 'tall, handsome and very charming' and Melanie enjoyed the pleasant and charming exchanges they would have together when he came in.

The pleasant exchanges increased over time and he asked Melanie out. She felt he was so respectful and kind that she had no hesitation in saying yes. They had the 'most amazing time' during the first few months and she could not believe that she had found true love twice in her lifetime. She felt very blessed.

Looking back on those months, Melanie became aware of some warning signs that she had not noticed at the time. Although he was very complimentary to her, he would often criticise others or belittle them. She had also found out that he did not own his house but was renting it. This in itself did not bother her, it was the fact that he had lied that troubled her. As time went on, the compliments lessened and the bullying and criticisms were turned towards her. Melanie became increasingly unhappy but felt it was difficult to leave as he would go from being very critical to being the most charming and, she felt at the time, loving person.

Melanie came to see me on her own as she came to the realisation that he did not care for her after all. She felt she had merely been a 'prop' to fulfil his needs and insecurities. Her needs, wants and desires did not matter.

The work that followed was similar to bereavement work. The pain and sadness Melanie felt was akin to some of the feelings she had when her husband had passed away. With some understanding, self-compassion and self-care, Melanie was able to move on from this relationship and be herself again.

If you are in a relationship with a narcissistic person and you would both like to work on the relationship, you will need to set firm boundaries. These may need to be discussed in a gentle yet firm way. The narcissistic partner may feel that their perfect veneer is being threatened and may feel very vulnerable because of this. This can be a challenging issue and you may wish to have the additional support of a qualified therapist to help you both make the changes necessary in your relationship.

Chapter 10

A client's perspective

'It takes a lot of courage to speak to a stranger about our inner selves'

Below is some of the feedback that I have received from clients who have worked with me over the years.

I was at the end, after 20 years I was mentally and physically broken. Our marriage had some particularly difficult times due to my army service but we got through. Now however it was a daily war of attrition, nothing I did was right. Meaningful communication was impossible. My anchor was now old enough to look after himself so I planned my escape. I had built our home with my own hands and there were a thousand other things I did not want to lose, mostly my wife. However it just seemed impossible. Sabine was genuinely a last throw of the dice.
We arrived for sessions in separate cars and at first none of it was easy. What was special for me was not only the way Sabine was able to translate the Venus and Mars language but to also find common ground. My wife and I began to understand a little bit about each other's issues and build on the common ground. At each session we seemed to build a bridge or take down a wall and it was all so natural. Sabine was our wonderful no nonsense, no gimmicks guide and interpreter.

Mr and Mrs. B. UK

My husband and I were supported by Sabine for a year where she helped us through the toughest year we have had. Throughout all sessions, she carefully supported conversations, helping us to feel comfortable within the session. She also managed those sessions when emotions were extremely high. She was excellent at helping each of us learn to really listen to and understand each other's view point which was not always an easy task. Sabine led each session using our requests to ensure that they were as beneficial as possible. She has helped us to look at many aspects of our relationship and provided us with skills and strategies needed that we will continue to use moving forwards. I never imagined to get to where we are today; a year on. It would not have been possible without Sabine and her guidance.
Thank you!

Mr and Mrs. G. UK

Thankyou for all your help over the last year, it has been really fundamental to how we re-built our relationship, and I personally have massively appreciated your non-judgemental approach and your general personal style. So thank you.

Mr and Mrs J.I UK

After our marriage broke down into consistent arguments, we sought the help of a relationship counsellor. Sabine provided a safe, secure and systematic assessment of our needs with warmth and respect. While in Sabine's practice and digital appointments, there was a safe and non-judgmental environment that nurtured open communication.

During this time, Sabine was flexible and reliable and was always available to meet our needs, no matter how frequent they were.
Sabine supported us to develop practical tools and techniques. The tools, techniques and understanding helped us, as a couple, to develop better communication during our sessions and in our relationship overall.
Together, we set relationship goals and strived towards them. Once we felt we had reached the end of our sessions, our marriage was better than it had ever been. Even after our main block of sessions were completed we felt the need to have the occasional session with Sabine - and she was more than happy to accommodate this.
There is no doubt that relationship counselling works, especially with the patience, understanding and warmth that Sabine so kindly provides. We are forever grateful!

Mr and Mrs. S. UK

For us having counselling had a way of exposing the truth of the pitfalls in our marriage when, at home, we could just carry on and deny what was really happening.

Mr and Mrs. J. UK

We first approached Sabine for Relationship counseling mid way through the pandemic at a time that it felt our relationship of 15 years had finally run its course. We had started a family but had lost 'us' in the process. Sabine helped us realise how busy life can be but that we still had to take time out for us as individuals and as a couple. She helped us look at our relationship and how we see each other in a completely new light. We no longer argue constantly but instead talk about the things that upset us and however busy life is, we make time for each other now. By no means are we out of the woods yet as we believe to make a relationship work, you will always need to put the effort in but Sabine has helped us realise and create the tools needed to enable us to do this together.

Sabine is such a warm person, it would feel as if a huge weight had been lifted after our sessions together. She has saved our relationship and for that we will be forever grateful.

Mr and Mrs. J. UK

Sabine provided us with a warm and welcoming environment which enabled us to be open and honest with each other. She made us feel comfortable and relaxed during the sessions.
Her guidance and advise helped us to find our way through our difficult time.

Mr and Mrs. L. UK

I was grateful to find Sabine toward the end of my long-distance relationship with my former partner who lives in London. We were able to meet remotely via Zoom and she created a calm, caring atmosphere for us to communicate. She was friendly, professional, and very accommodating. She was a fair mediator—always kind and gentle, but also challenging when it was needed.

Ms. K. USA

Sabine saved our marriage. Our relationship had reached a point where we thought counselling would probably just mediate an easier separation. Instead, in a safe space, we were able to express anger and disappointment, listen to each other, find forgiveness and even laugh. Sabine encouraged us to stop holding on to past anger, and instead to look forwards and plan what we wanted from our future together. Two years later we are still together, still listening to each other, still laughing.

Mr and Mrs. N. UK

Sabine was incredibly calm, showing much empathy for both sides of the story 'our marriage' We felt completely reassured and safe in the space and able to share how we felt. It has given us the head space to see each other's point of view, Sabine gave us some excercises which we have both worked with and continue to do so. This gave us both control of our situation and so making important steps back to a good marriage.

Mr and Mrs. T. UK

A letter from your therapist

'A final word...'

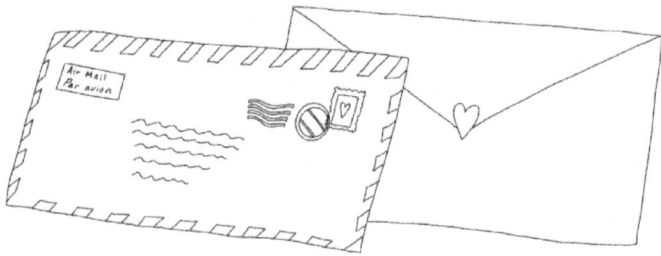

Dear Client,

Well done on completing this book.

You now have the tools and a better awareness of yourself and your relationship. This will help you create the relationship that you want and deserve.

This book was conceived because I feel passionate about helping people to reach their full potential. I have read many self-help books but felt that many were so laden with therapeutic words and theories that people might appreciate a no-nonsense, straight-talking book that would show and explain what would help a relationship and what would not.

A relationship and all of its various aspects is a large topic to cover in any one book but this book will give you the solid foundation you need to build a strong partnership. It may be that you will need more specific help in addition to this book, such as dealing with addiction. This book will enable you to gain the strength as an individual and as a couple to deal with these issues.

So, what is left for me to say?

Actually, something crucial to this process… and this is to nurture, value and respect yourself and your relationship for the rest of your life. As I mentioned earlier in the book, we are like plants. We need care and attention to thrive. It is not enough to have gotten your relationship to be the best it can be. You both need to, lovingly, keep that connection alive.

What may have felt like work at the start of this book, will now feel like a want and a pleasure, as the rewards of a happy and fulfilling relationship are great.

Now, go and have fun. Enjoy yourselves!

Sabine

Sabine

Appendix

UK

Domestic violence

Refuge – For Men, women and children against domestic violence

Freephone 24-Hour National Domestic Abuse Helpline: 0808 2000 247 or visit www.nationaldahelpline.org.uk (access live chat Mon-Fri 3-10pm)

Alcohol

Alcoholics Anonymous

Freephone 24-Hour Helpline: 0800 9177 650

Email: help@aamail.org

Live chat via website: www.alcoholics-anonymous.org.uk

Family

Supporting family issues, blended families, single parents and carers

Helpline: 0808 800 2222

askus@familylives.org.uk

Website: www.familylives.org.uk

USA

Domestic violence

Partnership Against Domestic Violence

Phone: (404) 870-9600

PADV's Crisis Lines (404) 873-1766 V/TTY

Alcohol

Alcoholics Anonymous

Website: www.aa.org/find-aa

Al-Anon and Ala-teen hotline line: 1-800-356-9996. Counsellors offer support to teens and adults who are negatively impacted by alcohol addiction, as well as resources to group therapy nearby for ongoing support.

Family

Family Help Center

Website: www.familyhelpcenter.net

24hr Family Helpline: 716.892.2172

Canada

Domestic violence

Family Violence Info Line: 780-310-1818

Battered Women's Support Services (BWSS) crisis line: 604-652-1867 / Toll free at 1-855-687-1868

SOS violence conjugale: 1-800-363-9010

Alcohol

Alcoholics Anonymous

Website: www.aa.org/find-aa

Family

PA Parent and Family Alliance

www.paparentandfamilyalliance.org

Parent Support Line at 888-273-2361

Australia

Domestic violence

Domestic Violence Helpline: Free call 1800 007 339

Alcohol

Alcohol and Drug Foundation (ADF) contact
Organisation

The Alcohol and Drug Foundation provides facts, resources and programs to help prevent alcohol and other drug harm in Australian communities. 1300 858 584

Family

Family Relationships Online: 1800 050 321

Strengthening family relationships

Helping families stay together

Assisting families through separation

Monday to Friday 8am to 8pm local time
Saturday 10am to 4pm local time
Closed Sundays and national public holidays

About the Author

Sabine Farren-Cox is a writer and licensed psychotherapist.

Born in the UK, having lived in a number of European countries and worked in a variety of environments including a university, a detention centre and various charities, she offers substantial experience, specialising in relationships and anxiety.

She currently runs her own private practice and lives on the Kent coast with her husband and children.

About the Illustrator

Caroline is an illustrator and animator and from a young age, has always had a keen interest in documenting the world around her through art.

Her work focusses on depicting everyday life with simplistic linework. After the completion of her Illustration and Animation degree, she went on to illustrate a number of her travels. Her skillset lies in creatively expressing the people and events that surround us all. Her work includes book illustration, bespoke logo and product design.

She divides her time between England and Canada.

Printed in Great Britain
by Amazon